12 LESSONS

jr. high

GRAPPLE

TACKLING TOUGH QUESTIONS ABOUT
GOD, OTHERS, AND ME

SMART DECISIONS

CD & DVD INCLUDED

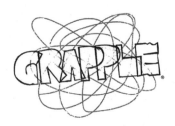

Grapple® Jr. High: Smart Decisions
Copyright © 2011 Group Publishing, Inc.

group.com
simplyyouthministry.com

ISBN 978-0-7644-7549-8

10 9 8 7 6 5 4 3 2 1   20 19 18 17 16 15 14 13 12 11

Printed in the United States of America.

TABLE OF CONTENTS

INTRODUCTION

GRAPPLE® JR. HIGH

Some of your students may already seem jaded about the Bible, and some of them have never cracked one open. Wherever your teenagers are in their spiritual journey, two things they all have in common are an inquisitive mind and a need for Christ-centered biblical depth. Grapple Jr. High is specifically designed to get junior highers grappling with tough topics in meaningful ways so they understand and own their faith. Each week, students engage with memorable Bible passages and characters, grapple with the issues that come to the surface, and discover a path that leads them straight to Jesus Christ.

During class, students follow the same schedule each week.

GRAPPLE SCHEDULE

5 MINUTES	HANG TIME
10 MINUTES	GRAPPLE CHAT
10-15 MINUTES	GRAPPLE TIME
20-25 MINUTES	TEAM TIME
10 MINUTES	TEAM REPORTS
5 MINUTES	PRAYER & CHALLENGE

Please note that times are approximate and should be flexible to fit your classroom needs.

WHAT HAPPENS?
GRAPPLE HANG TIME:

Kids enjoy snacks and friendship as they spend time getting to know each other as music plays in the background. Then play a three-minute countdown, included on your Grapple DVD, to let students know how much time they have until Grapple Hang Time is over. You can also use the countdowns to wrap up an activity in the lesson.

GRAPPLE CHAT:

Chat topics connect students to one another and to the Word of God. Two topics in each lesson are built on passages or characters from the Bible, and two topics challenge students to discuss their lives. Encourage students to choose one question from each of these categories. In each lesson, Questions 1 and 3 are the biblically based questions, and Questions 2 and 4 are the ones that tap into their personal experiences.

GRAPPLE TIME:

Grapple Time is the leader-led experience for your entire class. Grapple Time involves everyone in making discoveries; the experience helps students cultivate the desire to dig into the Bible for answers.

GRAPPLE TEAM TIME:

Students get into their Grapple Teams of six or fewer to dig into the Bible with the reproducible Grapple Team Guide.

Who leads a Grapple Team? If you have six or fewer students, have them stay together with you as the leader. If you have several Grapple Teams, try these ideas: Facilitate all the teams by moving from team to team, assign a student to be the team leader, or recruit adults or high school students to be team leaders.

GRAPPLE TEAM REPORTS:

Teams vote on how they want to report what they discovered during Grapple Team Time. Once teams are ready to report, they get with other teams that chose the other style of reporting. They then take turns reporting what they learned. If you have just one Grapple Team, consider dividing your team into two smaller groups to create and present reports.

GRAPPLE PRAYER AND CHALLENGE:

Kids choose, as a class, which prayer option they would like to do. After the class closes in prayer, give kids the weekly Grapple Challenge to live out their faith during the coming week.

ALLERGY ALERT

This guide may contain activities that include food. Be aware that some kids have food allergies that can be dangerous. Know the students in your class, and consult with parents about allergies their kids may have. Also be sure to carefully read food labels, as hidden ingredients can cause allergy-related problems.

THE SIXTH SENSE

HOW AM I SUPPOSED TO KNOW?

THE SIXTH SENSE

How Am I Supposed to Know?
The Point: The Holy Spirit Convicts Me
The Passages: Psalm 51:1-15; John 14:15-17; 16:5-15; Romans 3:22-23; 1 Thessalonians 4:7-8; 1 John 2:27-29

GET STARTED
Lesson 1. How Am I Supposed to Know?

GRAPPLE SCHEDULE

5 MINUTES	HANG TIME
10 MINUTES	GRAPPLE CHAT
10-15 MINUTES	GRAPPLE TIME
20-25 MINUTES	TEAM TIME
10 MINUTES	TEAM REPORTS
5 MINUTES	PRAYER & CHALLENGE

SUPPLIES
Bibles, Grapple DVD, DVD player, music CD, CD player, copy of the Grapple Team Guide for each person, paper, pens or pencils, 3x5 cards or slips of paper (three per student), bull's-eye

BIBLE BASIS FOR TEACHERS
The Passage: Psalm 51
David wrote this psalm after the prophet Nathan came to him and confronted him regarding his adultery with Bathsheba and his attempt to cover his sin by killing her husband Uriah (2 Samuel 11). In order to help David recognize his sin, Nathan told a parable of a greedy rich man who stole the one and only sheep that belonged to a poor man in order to serve a guest. In 2 Samuel 12:6, David said that the man who did what Nathan was referring to in his parable should *"repay four lambs to the poor man for the one he stole and for having no pity."* This verse refers to God's law in Exodus 22:1, which stated that a man must pay back four sheep if he stole one.

David's sentence of the man in Nathan's prophecy came true for himself: David and Bathsheba's firstborn son died, David's son Absalom incited a rebellion against him in which David was driven from Jerusalem, and Absalom slept with David's concubines (2 Samuel 12–16).

In Psalm 51 the Holy Spirit convicts David of his sin, and David eloquently proclaims his remorse and repentance. David's sin devastated him and his kingdom, but he sought forgiveness in a beautiful psalm of repentance. His plea for cleansing is an example for us all, who—like David—still sin.

How does this relate to the Grapple Question? Sometimes when we get caught up in sin, we may be blinded by our own selfishness. Sometimes we may even lie to ourselves and convince ourselves that what we're doing isn't wrong at all. David fell so deep into his own selfish ambition that he didn't recognize his sin even when it was laid out in front of him. Teenagers may wonder how they're supposed to know—due to ambiguous circumstances—whether a "sin" is actually a sin. This lesson will help them grapple with the gray areas in their own lives.

How does this connect to Jesus? Jesus said that he would send an Advocate to help his followers continue his ministry. One important thing this Advocate does is convict people of their sins (John 16:8). The Holy Spirit convicts Christians when they are disobeying God and brings them to a place of repentance. Because of the Holy Spirit, Christians can recognize their sin and their need for Jesus Christ to be a part of their lives.

GRAPPLE HANG TIME: 5 MINUTES
Play music as kids enjoy snacks and friendship, and then play an opening countdown from the Grapple DVD to wrap up Grapple Hang Time.

GRAPPLE CHAT: 10 MINUTES
Have students form pairs; if you have an uneven number of kids, it's OK to have one trio in the mix. Ask each group to chat about two of the four topics below that relate to today's grapple topic. (Answers in parentheses are samples.)

IN PAIRS
Chat 1: Find out what Enoch's prophecy, recorded in Jude, has to say. (God will judge and convict the ungodly, Jude 1:14-15)

Chat 2: Have you ever done something wrong without knowing it was wrong? How did that happen?

Chat 3: Find a verse in which Jesus describes himself as truth. (John 14:6)

Chat 4: Share three unusual facts about yourself.

GRAPPLE TIME: 10-15 MINUTES
Get Ready: Cue the Grapple DVD to the "The Twice-Thinker" clip.

Give each person three 3x5 cards (or slips of paper) and a pen or pencil.

Lead the entire class in the following:

Take a moment to think of three things teenagers your age do: one that's wrong, one that's fine, and one that might or might not be OK, depending on the situation. Pause. *Now, open your eyes, and write each action on a different 3x5 card.*

Collect and shuffle the cards, and ask the group to decide on body postures—such as standing, sitting, raising one arm, and so on—to represent wrong, right, and maybe. Let students practice each position, and then read each idea aloud, giving kids time to decide if it's a "wrong," "right," or "maybe" action. Allow for discussion whenever disagreement arises.

TELL ALL

How did you decide whether an action was wrong, right, or maybe? What situations do teenagers face that call for actions in the "maybe" category? When you've needed to decide if an action is right or wrong, what decision-making methods have you tried or have you seen others try? What worked well, and what didn't?

IN PAIRS

When have you been in a situation where you just didn't know what was the right thing to do? How did you handle it?

Show the "The Twice-Thinker" clip on the Grapple DVD.

Sometimes the right decision is clear: You've learned the truth from your parents, teachers, friends, the Bible, or experience. Other times, it seems you could go either way. It's complicated, tricky, and downright confusing. What do you do then? How are you supposed to know? Let's grapple with that!

GRAPPLE TEAM TIME: 20-25 MINUTES

Break into Grapple Teams. Encourage Grapple Team leaders to check in with kids about their week. Grapple Team leaders will facilitate discussion, using the Grapple Team Guide on pages 6-8. Afterward, students will report what they learned.

GRAPPLE TEAM REPORTS: 10 MINUTES

At the end of Grapple Team Time, match Grapple Teams that chose Option 1 with Grapple Teams that chose Option 2 from page 8. Have teams present their reports.

(If you have an uneven number of teams, simply form one group of three teams for the presentations. If you have only two Grapple Teams, simply do the presentations one team at a time.)

GRAPPLE PRAYER AND CHALLENGE: 5 MINUTES

Read the Grapple Prayer options. Have the class choose one prayer option that everyone will do. Allow students time to pray about what they discovered. Then close in prayer.

Get Ready: For Option 2, affix the bull's-eye to the far wall, and distribute paper to students.

Option 1: Letter Prayers
Write a letter to Jesus. Tell him what you know is true about him and what you're unsure about; ask for his strength and help in developing a deeper trust in him.

Option 2: Marksman, Markswoman
Make paper airplanes, and take turns throwing the airplanes at the bull's-eye. Walk to wherever your airplane lands and pray to God about one way you miss the mark in your life. Relate what you say to what you learned today.

GRAPPLE CHALLENGE
If you follow Jesus, God the Father has already fulfilled Jesus' request to send you the Holy Spirit, who will never leave you. The Spirit of God is with you, guiding you, helping you know wrong from right even when it's complicated. That's quite a gift! This week I challenge you: Each time you leave your home, ask the Holy Spirit to go with you and help you know what to do. The more you ask, the more the Spirit will show you the truth.

WEEKLY GRAPPLE CONNECTION
Grapple Question: How Am I Supposed to Know?
Kids Learn: The Holy Spirit Convicts Me
Dig Into the Bible: Psalm 51

Every day, you're faced with parenting decisions. And as your teenager gets older, those decisions can seem more and more complicated. It can be hard to know if you should intervene and guide your junior higher, or if you should stay quiet and let your teenager experience the natural consequences of his or her actions. It's complicated, tricky, and downright confusing.

The good news is that God sent the Holy Spirit, who will never leave you. You don't have to navigate these tricky parenting waters alone—you have the Spirit of God guiding you and helping you know what's best for your child even when it's complicated. That's quite a gift! Tap into this awesome resource this week by asking God to help you understand and pay attention to what the Holy Spirit has to say to you. You never have to feel alone again.

- -

GRAPPLE TEAM GUIDE LESSON 1
In your Grapple Team, use this guide to grapple with today's question.

Sit in a circle with your team, and take turns sharing one thing you know for sure is either right or wrong, until you've either exhausted what you know or you've been at it for two minutes. Go!

IN PAIRS
Did you hear anything that someone else knows for sure that you (a) didn't know or (b) disagree with? What? How do you know what you know? On a scale of 1 to 10, how confident do you feel about what you know? Explain your rating.

Read Romans 3:22-23

Based on this passage, write a definition for *sin*.

_____

_____

_____

What does sin have to do with how you know right from wrong?

_____

_____

_____

Sometimes people question whether a particular action is a sin or not. Let's see what the Bible says about how you can know what's right and what's wrong.

Read John 14:15-17; 16:5-15; and 1 Thessalonians 4:7-8

Write words or phrases Jesus uses to describe the Holy Spirit.

_____

_____

_____

What does the Holy Spirit have to do with knowing right from wrong? If the Holy Spirit is always with us as followers of Jesus, then why do people keep sinning?

_____

_____

_____

IN PAIRS

Including what you just read, what do you know about the Holy Spirit? When, if ever, have you sensed the Holy Spirit giving you guidance? What are ways we can better pay attention to the Holy Spirit's guidance?

Read Psalm 51:1-15 and 1 John 2:27-29

What comfort can these passages offer you? How would you explain this good news to someone who's not here today?

_____

_____

_____

In 1 John 2:28 we're encouraged to *"remain in fellowship with Christ."* How do we do that? How can the Holy Spirit help us?

_____

_____

_____

GRAPPLE TEAM REPORTS

With your team, choose one of the options below to report what you discovered.

Get Ready: For Option 2, make sure students have paper and pens or pencils.

Option 1: Proverb It
Look through the book of Proverbs and find one verse that best connects to what you learned today. If you have enough time, consider finding additional verses.

Option 2: Preach It; Practice It
Create a short instruction manual titled "Practice What You Preach." Come up with at least 10 ways everyone can put today's lesson into practice this next week.

HOW AM I SUPPOSED TO KNOW?

John 16:13a
When the Spirit of truth comes, he will guide you into all truth.

GRAPPLE CHAT
Chat 1: Find out what Enoch's prophecy, recorded in Jude, has to say.

Chat 2: Have you ever done something wrong without knowing it was wrong? How did that happen?

Chat 3: Find a verse in which Jesus describes himself as truth.

Chat 4: Share three unusual facts about yourself.

GRAPPLE CHALLENGE
Each time you leave your home this week, ask the Holy Spirit to go with you and help you know what to do.

NOTES:
_____

_____

_____

_____

_____

_____

_____

_____

_____

_____

THE SIXTH SENSE

WHAT DOES GOD WANT?

THE SIXTH SENSE

What Does God Want?
The Point: The Holy Spirit Guides Me
The Passages: Psalm 139:1-18; 143:10; Acts 16:6-10; 1 Corinthians 2:10-12; Galatians 5:16-25

GET STARTED
Lesson 2. What Does God Want?

GRAPPLE SCHEDULE

5 MINUTES	HANG TIME
10 MINUTES	GRAPPLE CHAT
10-15 MINUTES	GRAPPLE TIME
20-25 MINUTES	TEAM TIME
10 MINUTES	TEAM REPORTS
5 MINUTES	PRAYER & CHALLENGE

SUPPLIES
Bibles, Grapple DVD, DVD player, music CD, CD player, copy of the Grapple Team Guide for each person, paper, pens or pencils, copies of maps printed from a mapping website

BIBLE BASIS FOR TEACHERS
The Passage: Acts 16:6-10
In this passage Paul and Silas are at the beginning of a missionary journey through Asia and Greece. The Holy Spirit was guiding Paul and Silas along the way, so much so that the Spirit was preventing the missionaries from preaching in certain places. When Paul and Silas tried to go north into the province of Bithynia, located in the northwest portion of Asia Minor (Turkey today), the Holy Spirit stopped them and guided them elsewhere. That same evening, Paul received a vision from the Holy Spirit guiding them to Macedonia. Paul and Silas obeyed the message, crossed the sea, and preached the message of Jesus to the Macedonians.

How does this relate to the Grapple Question? Sometimes you hear Christians say, "God told me to do this" or "God said that he wanted me to do that." Teenagers may wonder why God doesn't speak to them directly. Every Christian wonders at some point what God wants from him or her and what God has planned for his or her life. The Holy Spirit serves as a great guide if we allow him to lead (see John 16:13). Paul didn't have his whole trip planned out by a travel agent before he left on his missionary journeys. In fact, Paul relied on the guidance of the Holy Spirit to lead him where God wanted him to go.

How does this connect to Jesus? Jesus constantly relied on the guidance of the Holy Spirit. After his baptism, Jesus was led into the wilderness by the Holy Spirit where he was tempted (Luke 4:1-2). The Scriptures say that Jesus was also led by the Holy Spirit while he preached and performed miracles (Luke 4:14, 18-19). Before ascending into heaven, Jesus promised his disciples that they would be filled with the Holy Spirit and the Holy Spirit would lead them to spread the gospel *"to the ends of the earth" (Acts 1:8).*

GRAPPLE HANG TIME: 5 MINUTES
Play music as kids enjoy snacks and friendship, and then play an opening countdown from the Grapple DVD to wrap up Grapple Hang Time.

GRAPPLE CHAT: 10 MINUTES
Have students form pairs; if you have an uneven number of kids, it's OK to have one trio in the mix. Ask each group to chat about two of the four topics below that relate to today's grapple topic. (Answers in parentheses are samples.)

IN PAIRS
Chat 1: What did God use to guide the Israelites through the desert as they escaped from Egypt? (A pillar of cloud by day and pillar of fire by night, Exodus 13:21-22)

Chat 2: What other cities and states have you visited? Which did you enjoy the most, and why?

Chat 3: According to Zachariah's prophecy in Luke, what will the morning light from heaven do? (Guide us to the path of peace, Luke 1:78-79)

Chat 4: Where do you want to go to college, and why? And if not college, what do you want to do right after high school, and why?

GRAPPLE TIME: 10-15 MINUTES
Get Ready: Cue the Grapple DVD to the "The Holy Spirit Will..." clip.

Lead the entire class in the following:

Find a partner, and choose who will be a leader first. Pause. *Leaders, think of three things you'd like to see your partner do right now, right here. For example, stand on one foot, do jumping jacks, sing a song.* Pause as kids think. *Got them? Your job is to get your partner to do those things without speaking and without doing the activities yourself. Followers, you can ask only yes-or-no questions. Leaders, you can only nod or shake your head to respond. After one minute, you'll trade roles. Ready? Go!*

TELL ALL
When you were a leader, how successful were you at leading your partner? When you were a follower, how did you feel about trying to follow your leader? What

made this activity difficult? What would have made it easier? Describe the kind of leader you'd like to follow.

IN PAIRS
When have you tried to follow people who weren't clear about what they wanted? What happened in those situations?

Show the "The Holy Spirit Will..." clip on the Grapple DVD.

It's really difficult—and sometimes impossible—to follow leaders who don't clearly communicate what they want. Unfortunately, some people feel that way about God. Just what does God want? How are you supposed to know? And if you don't know, how can you follow God at all? Let's grapple with that today.

GRAPPLE TEAM TIME: 20-25 MINUTES
Break into Grapple Teams. Encourage Grapple Team leaders to check in with kids about their week. Grapple Team leaders will facilitate discussion, using the Grapple Team Guide on pages 16-18. Afterward, students will report what they learned.

GRAPPLE TEAM REPORTS: 10 MINUTES
At the end of Grapple Team Time, match Grapple Teams that chose Option 1 with Grapple Teams that chose Option 2 from page 18. Have teams present their reports.

(If you have an uneven number of teams, simply form one group of three teams for the presentations. If you have only two Grapple Teams, simply do the presentations one team at a time.)

GRAPPLE PRAYER AND CHALLENGE: 5 MINUTES
Read the Grapple Prayer options. Have the class choose one prayer option that everyone will do. Allow students time to pray about what they discovered. Then close in prayer.

Get Ready: For Option 2, distribute copies of maps printed from a mapping website.

Option 1: Psalms That Pray
Get comfortable, preferably sitting apart from each other. Look through the book of Psalms and find a psalm that connects with a situation you're facing right now. Read the psalm quietly as a prayer to God.

Option 2: Roadmap of Wisdom
Look at a map, and consider all the different roads and highways and streets featured on that map. Pray for God's guidance, wisdom, and direction in your life, and ask God for strength in following the path and plan he has created for you.

GRAPPLE CHALLENGE

How often do you notice your shadow? It's with you whenever light shines, but it's easy to ignore. If you love Jesus, the Holy Spirit is with you always—but you have to notice the Holy Spirit and take time to listen. What God wants is you—a loving, fulfilling relationship with you. This week, make time for a two-way relationship with God. Don't just toss your prayer requests at God; listen to the Holy Spirit. Set aside time to read the Bible, and ask the Holy Spirit to teach you to do God's will. Pray before you make decisions. And wait for guidance. Seek God, and you will discover that God wants to talk to you way more than you knew.

WEEKLY GRAPPLE CONNECTION

Grapple Question: What Does God Want?
Kids Learn: The Holy Spirit Guides Me
Dig Into the Bible: Acts 16:6-10

Have you ever had to follow directions that were really unclear? Maybe your boss didn't explain expectations upfront, leaving room for confusion about your assignment. Or maybe some friends gave some vague directions to their house, causing you to wind aimlessly around an unfamiliar part of town.

It's really difficult—and sometimes impossible—to follow leaders who don't clearly communicate what they want. Unfortunately, some people feel that way about God. Just what does God want? How are we supposed to know?

God sent the Holy Spirit to help us figure out stuff like that. We can read the Bible and ask God through prayer to make his directions clear to us. But that requires some effort. This week set an example for your teenager by seeking God's will—through prayer and Bible study—for a decision you have to make. Discuss with your teenager how you feel about this process—does this come easily to you, or does it take some effort? Encourage your child to join you on this adventure of figuring out what God wants for you and your family.

- -

GRAPPLE TEAM GUIDE LESSON 2

In your Grapple Team, use this guide to grapple with today's question.

Tell your team how you've experienced God as a leader in your life, using just one or two words (*clear, confusing, good, frustrating, quiet,* or *loud,* for example). Explain your description.

IN PAIRS

Share at least one thing you think God wants and why you think God wants that. What has been your experience in trying to do what God wants? What was hard? What was easy?

The Apostle Paul had to listen carefully to know what God wanted him to do and where God wanted him to go. Take a look at one experience Paul and Silas had as they spread the good news about Jesus.

Read Acts 16:6-10

Read this passage again as you stand up and walk together as a group. Each time the Spirit prevented Paul and Silas from going someplace, change direction.

How did the Holy Spirit guide Paul and Silas?

_____

_____

_____

IN PAIRS

How do you think the Holy Spirit communicates with people today?

Read Psalm 139:1-18

Write or draw your response to this passage on a separate piece of paper. Include how it makes you feel, how it affects your relationship with God, and what you think it has to do with what God wants.

Read 1 Corinthians 2:10-12 and Psalm 143:10

What in these passages surprises you? How can you know if your thoughts are actually God's thoughts revealed to you by the Holy Spirit? When has guidance from the Spirit made a difference in your daily life?

_____

_____

_____

Read Galatians 5:16-25

Notice what the Spirit wants and what the sinful nature wants. What are some things you can do to let the Spirit guide your life?

_____

_____

_____

IN PAIRS

Now that you've spent some time in God's Word, what do you think God wants, and why? What are obstacles that could keep you from doing what God wants, and why? What's one way to overcome one obstacle?

GRAPPLE TEAM REPORTS

With your team, choose one of the options below to report what you discovered.

Option 1: Text It

Write a 140-character text message that you could send to a friend or family member explaining what you learned today.

Option 2: Dialogue

Create a scene from your everyday life that includes dialogue involving everyone on your team (or several sample conversations) to demonstrate what you've learned today.

WHAT DOES GOD WANT?
(STUDENT)

John 16:13a
When the Spirit of truth comes, he will guide you into all truth.

GRAPPLE CHAT
Chat 1: What did God use to guide the Israelites through the desert as they escaped from Egypt?

Chat 2: What other cities and states have you visited? Which did you enjoy the most, and why?

Chat 3: According to Zachariah's prophecy in Luke, what will the morning light from heaven do?

Chat 4: Where do you want to go to college, and why? And if not college, what do you want to do right after high school, and why?

GRAPPLE CHALLENGE
Go to the Bible every day with this question for God: "What do you want me to do?"

NOTES:

_____

_____

_____

_____

_____

_____

_____

_____

THE SIXTH SENSE

WHAT'S UP WITH THE "SHEPHERD"?

THE SIXTH SENSE

What's Up With the "Shepherd"?
The Point: The Holy Spirit Comforts Me
The Passages: Psalm 23; Romans 5:1-5; 8:26-27; Ephesians 1:13-14

GET STARTED
Lesson 3. What's Up With the "Shepherd"?

GRAPPLE SCHEDULE

5 MINUTES	HANG TIME
10 MINUTES	GRAPPLE CHAT
10-15 MINUTES	GRAPPLE TIME
20-25 MINUTES	TEAM TIME
10 MINUTES	TEAM REPORTS
5 MINUTES	PRAYER & CHALLENGE

SUPPLIES
Bibles, Grapple DVD, DVD player, music CD, CD player, copy of the Grapple Team Guide for each person, paper, pens or pencils, poster board, markers

BIBLE BASIS FOR TEACHERS
The Passage: Psalm 23

It's easy to look at this psalm as a nice, peaceful recitation written during a time of safety and comfort. However, it may have been written during a time of crisis—a time when danger was all around and David needed God's help. But instead of complaining about his situation, David took the opportunity to express his trust in the Lord. He confidently proclaimed that God would care for him all of his days.

David begins the psalm with an image of God as a good shepherd. The things David describes in Psalm 23:1-4 are all things a good shepherd gives his sheep: food, water, guidance, and protection. The second image in this psalm runs through Psalm 23:5—the image of a good host who provides for a guest's needs, even in the face of danger.

The final verse gives assurance: Not only will God provide for us in particular crises, but God also will give us this same kind of care all through our lives. God can work in any crisis we face, and God will give us all we need to work through it and come out honoring him.

How does this relate to the Grapple Question? The shepherd metaphor has lost some of its power since King David's time, or even since Jesus' day. Junior highers may not be familiar with the protection imagery connected to shepherds; some kids may be curious about the shepherd imagery. Still, other students may

be asking a deeper question. They wonder where God is during their time of need. Furthermore, they may wonder how God could possibly provide them with the comfort they need to make it through their daily battles.

How does this connect to Jesus? The Bible promises us that because of Jesus, God will give us comfort (2 Corinthians 1:3-7). The Holy Spirit provides us with the comfort we need to endure the sufferings that the world throws at us. Jesus knew that those who chose to follow him would need a comforter, and the Holy Spirit provides that comfort.

GRAPPLE HANG TIME: 5 MINUTES
Play music as kids enjoy snacks and friendship, and then play an opening countdown from the Grapple DVD to wrap up Grapple Hang Time.

GRAPPLE CHAT: 10 MINUTES
Have students form pairs; if you have an uneven number of kids, it's OK to have one trio in the mix. Ask each group to chat about two of the four topics below that relate to today's grapple topic. (Answers in parentheses are samples.)

IN PAIRS
Chat 1: Which Israelite patriarch's wife was originally a shepherdess? (Jacob's wife Rachel, Genesis 29:9)

Chat 2: What was your the favorite childhood toy, and when was the last time you played with that toy?

Chat 3: Discover what the tribes of Israel said to David at Hebron. (The Lord told you that you would shepherd Israel, 2 Samuel 5:1-2)

Chat 4: Have you ever seen a shepherd in a field with sheep? If so, where?

GRAPPLE TIME: 10-15 MINUTES
Get Ready: Cue the Grapple DVD to the "A Lost Sheep" clip. Help kids form two teams, and give each team a piece of paper and a pen or pencil.

Lead the entire class in the following:

As a team, list at least 10 roles a person could play in life. Teacher, friend, and neighbor are some examples. Use your creativity so that we won't have lots of repeats. Give teams a couple of minutes to create their lists. *Now take turns reading something from your team's list to complete this phrase, "My [blank—first team's role] is my [blank—second team's role]." So if team one wrote "teacher" and team two wrote "friend," the sentence would read, "My teacher is my friend." Then we'll vote to see whether you think the sentence makes sense.*

Make sure each person gets a chance to read a role from the team's list, and allow for discussion as necessary between sentences. (You can reverse sentences, too, and see if they make sense that way.) If you have time and the group has enjoyed this activity, you can repeat the activity with one team reading its list from the bottom up.

TELL ALL
How can knowing someone's role help you to know the person better? What if you didn't know anything about someone's role—for example, a very specialized kind of scientist? How would that change your ability to know the person?

IN PAIRS
What might "The Lord is my shepherd" tell you about God? What does it mean to you?

Show the "A Lost Sheep" clip on the Grapple DVD.

When you introduce people to one another, you can give them something to talk about if you give them a little extra information, like, "This friend is on my soccer team." The Bible describes the Lord as our shepherd, which is great if you know what that means. Sheep and shepherds were really common in the region where the Bible was written but aren't so common for most of us in the 21st century. So what's up with the "Shepherd"? Let's grapple with that.

GRAPPLE TEAM TIME: 20-25 MINUTES
Break into Grapple Teams. Encourage Grapple Team leaders to check in with kids about their week. Grapple Team leaders will facilitate discussion, using the Grapple Team Guide on pages 26-28. Afterward, students will report what they learned.

GRAPPLE TEAM REPORTS: 10 MINUTES
At the end of Grapple Team Time, match Grapple Teams that chose Option 1 with Grapple Teams that chose Option 2 from page 28. Have teams present their reports.

(If you have an uneven number of teams, simply form one group of three teams for the presentations. If you have only two Grapple Teams, simply do the presentations one team at a time.)

GRAPPLE PRAYER AND CHALLENGE: 5 MINUTES
Read the Grapple Prayer options. Have the class choose one prayer option that everyone will do. Allow students time to pray about what they discovered. Then close in prayer.

Option 1: Lectio Divina
Get comfortable, preferably sitting apart from each other. Read a Bible passage aloud, and then remain in silence for a few minutes and think about the verses. Close your eyes and breathe deeply. Then read aloud Romans 8:35-39, slowly and with feeling. Then read it two more times the same way. Finally, allow a few minutes to silently bask in God's love.

Option 2: You Are; I Am

Find a partner to pray with. God gave us the Bible so we could know him and so we could know who we really are. Take turns each praying a one-sentence prayer that starts, "God, you are...." Then take turns each praying a one-sentence prayer that starts with the words: "Because of your love for me, God, I am...."

GRAPPLE CHALLENGE

While you probably didn't come today expecting to be told that you're a sheep in need of a shepherd, I hope that image means so much more to you now. I encourage you to hold on to the image of God as your Shepherd this week. When you lie down to rest, remember that you can be at peace because God watches out for you. When you're sad, remember that you're not alone because God is with you. When you drink or eat, remember the feast God has prepared for you. Our Shepherd is our good and loving God!

WEEKLY GRAPPLE CONNECTION

Grapple Question: What's Up With the "Shepherd"?
Kids Learn: The Holy Spirit Comforts Me
Dig Into the Bible: Psalm 23

When was the last time you felt depressed and hopeless? We all go through stressful times in our lives. God can seem far away when we are discouraged and lonely.

Sometimes the only way to make it through those times is to cling to the assurance that God is with us. Find a comforting passage to read to get you through hard times. Post it in your home for everyone to be encouraged. Try Psalm 23, which describes God as our Shepherd who brings us peace and rest. You might even want to memorize that passage so you can recall it when you need it. Remember that you can be at peace because God watches out for you— our Shepherd is our good and loving God!

- -

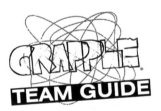

GRAPPLE TEAM GUIDE LESSON 3

In your Grapple Team, use this guide to grapple with today's question.

Think of a time you needed comfort. Perhaps a friend moved away, maybe couldn't do something as well as you wanted to, or maybe a pet died. What helped you feel better? Now think of your own sign language to represent the person, place, or thing that comforted you. Got it? Turn to a partner. On the count of three, show your sign language, and then take turns guessing what comforted your partner.

IN PAIRS

How was that person, place, or thing able to comfort you? When have you felt comforted by God? How did you experience God's comfort?

Let's get right to the heart of today's topic.

Read Psalm 23

1		
2		
3		
4		
5		
6		

In the left column, write what you think each verse means. What does it mean that the Lord is your shepherd and you have all that you need? Hint: It will help if you think about what life might be like if you were a sheep!

Then work as a team to rewrite the psalm in the right column, using language and images that make sense to you in your world today. God wants to have a real-life relationship with you now, so pray and ask God for guidance on what kinds of descriptive words will make sense to you here and now.

IN PAIRS

How do you feel about God as your shepherd now? How does it make more sense? What difference can this knowledge make to your life this week?

Read Romans 5:1-5; 8:26-27; and Ephesians 1:13-14

As you read each passage, write down what the Holy Spirit does for us.

_____

_____

_____

Based on these passages, describe the relationship God wants to have with you.

_____

_____

_____

How do these passages support the picture of God recorded in Psalm 23?

_____

_____

_____

GRAPPLE TEAM REPORTS

With your team, choose one of the options below to report what you discovered.

Get Ready: For Option 2, distribute poster board and markers.

Option 1: ABCs

Write the ABCs of what you learned today: a statement that starts with an A, a statement that starts with a B, and so on. Try to go as far into the alphabet as you can—even all the way to Z.

Option 2: Chart It

Use poster board and markers to create a chart or poster that illustrates what you learned today. Be sure to include some biblical facts and also some information about how your conclusion has affected your own lives.

WHAT'S UP WITH THE "SHEPHERD"?
(STUDENT)

John 16:13a
When the Spirit of truth comes, he will guide you into all truth.

GRAPPLE CHAT
Chat 1: Which Israelite patriarch's wife was originally a shepherdess?

Chat 2: What was your the favorite childhood toy, and when was the last time you played with that toy?

Chat 3: Discover what the tribes of Israel said to David at Hebron.

Chat 4: Have you ever seen a shepherd in a field with sheep? If so, where?

GRAPPLE CHALLENGE
Remember the image of the shepherd every time you go to bed this week: God gives you rest, protects you, and provides for you.

NOTES:

_____

_____

_____

_____

_____

_____

_____

_____

_____

THE SIXTH SENSE

WHAT IF I'M SCARED?

THE SIXTH SENSE

What if I'm Scared?
The Point: The Holy Spirit Empowers Me
The Passages: Acts 27:13-26; Romans 8:1-2, 5-6, 9-11, 38-39; 2 Timothy 1:7

GET STARTED
Lesson 4. What if I'm Scared?

GRAPPLE SCHEDULE

5 MINUTES	HANG TIME
10 MINUTES	GRAPPLE CHAT
10-15 MINUTES	GRAPPLE TIME
20-25 MINUTES	TEAM TIME
10 MINUTES	TEAM REPORTS
5 MINUTES	PRAYER & CHALLENGE

SUPPLIES
Bibles, Grapple DVD, DVD player, music CD, CD player, copy of the Grapple Team Guide for each person, paper, pens or pencils

BIBLE BASIS FOR TEACHERS
The Passage: Acts 27:13-26
After the Apostle Paul's imprisonment in Caesarea, he boarded a ship for Rome to stand trial before Caesar. When the ship's voyage was delayed by the wind direction, it became apparent that the crew and passengers wouldn't reach Rome before the bad winter weather arrived. Paul advised that they stay put for the winter, but those in charge decided to keep going to a better port. When a favorable wind started to blow, they sailed on but were soon blown off course in a terrible storm.

We don't know exactly what the sailors did with the ropes to try to keep the ship together. They may have wrapped them around the hull in an attempt to keep it from coming apart, or they may have tied ropes from bow to stern to try to avoid having the ship break in two in the mighty waves.

After nearly two weeks of this storm, all aboard the ship must have felt certain that they were going to die. But the message Paul received from God told them otherwise. Paul was obviously confident that they would all be saved, but we don't know how well the others received his message. We do know that when Paul prayed for them and urged them to eat as they approached land, they were encouraged—all 276 of them!

How does this relate to the Grapple Question? All kinds of things scare us. Junior highers may be afraid of not being accepted, or failing a test, or looking foolish in front of the "in" crowd. Paul was in the midst of a major storm. Everyone on that boat was afraid, but Paul provided them with hope. Sometimes teenagers get so scared that they don't know what to do with themselves. This Grapple Question will help students face their fears by trusting in the Holy Spirit.

How does this connect to Jesus? Jesus frequently told his disciples and the people around him not to be afraid (Luke 5:10; John 6:20). Fear is a normal human reaction, but it has the ability to take over. God wants us to trust in him—and not in ourselves or our own ability to overcome difficulties. The Holy Spirit provides us with protection from Satan and his schemes. With the power of the Holy Spirit, we can face our fears head-on and be victorious.

GRAPPLE HANG TIME: 5 MINUTES
Play music as kids enjoy snacks and friendship, and then play an opening countdown from the Grapple DVD to wrap up Grapple Hang Time.

GRAPPLE CHAT: 10 MINUTES
Have students form pairs; if you have an uneven number of kids, it's OK to have one trio in the mix. Ask each group to chat about two of the four topics below that relate to today's grapple topic. (Answers in parentheses are samples.)

IN PAIRS
Chat 1: Find out why God told Joshua not be afraid or discouraged. (God told Joshua to be strong and courageous because God was with him, Joshua 1:6-9)

Chat 2: Talk about a time when you conquered a fear—what the fear was and how you conquered it.

Chat 3: Discover what the first two chapters of Luke tell us the angels said when they appeared to people. ("Don't be afraid," Luke 1:13, 30; and 2:10)

Chat 4: What's the scariest amusement park ride you've been on, and would you ride it again? Why or why not?

GRAPPLE TIME: 10-15 MINUTES
Get Ready: Cue the Grapple DVD to the clip titled "The Standoff." Give each Grapple Team paper and a pen or pencil.

Lead the entire class in the following:

Life can be scary. Work in your Grapple Team to come up with a top 10 list of things that scare you or people your age. Someone on your team will read your list for the rest of us, starting with number 10, the least scary thing, and working up to number 1, the scariest. Try to bring some humor into this, because sometimes life is scary, and we all need to laugh more.

When teams are ready, have them read the lists. Take them seriously, but enjoy a few good laughs together, too!

IN PAIRS

What did you notice about the fears on these lists? For example, were items on the lists similar or different? How can humor help you handle your fears? What else helps you when you feel afraid? How has God helped you handle your fears?

TELL ALL

On a scale of 1 to 10, how often do you feel afraid? What would you say is your biggest fear? How do you handle it?

Show the clip titled "The Standoff" on the Grapple DVD.

Even the strongest, bravest person feels afraid sometimes. We all do. It's part of being human. So where does God fit in? Does God care? Can God help? What do we do if we're scared? Let's grapple with that!

GRAPPLE TEAM TIME: 20-25 MINUTES

Break into Grapple Teams. Encourage Grapple Team leaders to check in with kids about their week. Grapple Team leaders will facilitate discussion, using the Grapple Team Guide on pages 36-37. Afterward, students will report what they learned.

GRAPPLE TEAM REPORTS: 10 MINUTES

At the end of Grapple Team Time, match Grapple Teams that chose Option 1 with Grapple Teams that chose Option 2 from page 38. Have teams present their reports.

(If you have an uneven number of teams, simply form one group of three teams for the presentations. If you have only two Grapple Teams, simply do the presentations one team at a time.)

GRAPPLE PRAYER AND CHALLENGE: 5 MINUTES

Read the Grapple Prayer options. Have the class choose one prayer option that everyone will do. Allow students time to pray about what they discovered. Then close in prayer.

Option 1: Prayer Partners

Find a partner to pray with. Talk about troubles you currently face, especially anything connected to today's lesson. Then pray for each other to be able to see your situation from God's perspective.

Option 2: Word Prayers

Take a quiet moment to consider what you know about God. Then prayerfully call out one or two words that describe who God is, such as Comforter, Protector, Provider, or Shepherd.

GRAPPLE CHALLENGE

Yes, life can be scary. But God is bigger, stronger, and more powerful than anything that scares us. Not even death can stop God! This week, anytime you start to feel afraid, nervous, anxious, worried, or however you want to put it, ask the Holy Spirit to fill you with power and courage. With all of God's power available to you, there's no need to be stopped by fear.

WEEKLY GRAPPLE CONNECTION

Grapple Question: What if I'm Scared?
Kids Learn: The Holy Spirit Empowers Me
Dig Into the Bible: Acts 27:13-26

Over dinner tonight, have a conversation about what each family member fears. You might start out with lighter topics, like spiders and heights. But also encourage each person to go a little deeper by sharing a fear of loneliness, failure, or death, for example.

Even the strongest, bravest person feels afraid sometimes. We all do; it's part of being human. But God is bigger, stronger, and more powerful than anything that scares us. Not even death can stop God! Continue your family conversation and ask what each person can do to lean on God when he or she is afraid, nervous, or anxious. With God's Spirit available to you, there's no need to be afraid.

- -

GRAPPLE TEAM GUIDE LESSON 4

In your Grapple Team, use this guide to grapple with today's question.

On the count of three, show your team your best "scared" face. One, two, three, boo! Now show your team your best "confident" face. Now let's go to the Bible and find some truth to make us feel confident—even when we're scared.

Read Romans 8:38-39

In a few words, sum up these verses. Have you ever felt afraid that God wouldn't love you? What comfort does this passage offer?

_____

_____

_____

Read Romans 8:1-2, 5-6, 9-11

Describe the Holy Spirit and what he does.

_____

_____

_____

IN PAIRS

The Bible says that the same Spirit who raised Jesus from the dead lives in you. What's something you're hoping the Spirit can "raise from the dead" in you? The Spirit is powerful! How have you experienced that power when you were afraid?

Read Acts 27:13-26

On a blank sheet of paper, draw a picture of a time you were afraid that things weren't going to turn out well for you.

An angel came and reassured Paul that things would be OK. How has God reassured you of his presence at times you were afraid?

_____

_____

_____

IN PAIRS

What are some of your biggest fears about your future? How can the Holy Spirit empower you in those situations?

And one final word...

Read 2 Timothy 1:7

Rewrite this verse in your own words.

_____

_____

_____

GRAPPLE TEAM REPORTS

With your team, choose one of the options below to report what you discovered.

Option 1: Condense It
If you had to summarize today's lesson in only five words, what would they be? As a team, choose the words carefully, and be prepared to explain why you chose them.

Option 2: Instant Object Lesson
Use whatever you can find around you to create some instant object lessons that explain what you learned today. Get creative!

WHAT IF I'M SCARED?
(STUDENT)

John 16:13a
When the Spirit of truth comes, he will guide you into all truth.

GRAPPLE CHAT
Chat 1: Find out why God told Joshua not be afraid or discouraged.

Chat 2: Talk about a time when you conquered a fear—what the fear was and how you conquered it.

Chat 3: Discover what the first two chapters of Luke tell us the angels said when they appeared to people.

Chat 4: What's the scariest amusement park ride you've been on, and would you ride it again? Why or why not?

GRAPPLE CHALLENGE
This week, whenever you're afraid or nervous, ask the Holy Spirit to give you strength and courage.

NOTES:
_____

_____

_____

_____

_____

_____

_____

_____

TO DO OR NOT TO DO?

WHAT IF EVERYONE'S DOING IT?

TO DO OR NOT TO DO?

What if Everyone's Doing It?
The Point: I Will Honor God
The Passages: Matthew 13:53-58; Mark 3:1-6; Romans 12:1-2; Colossians 3:1-15; 2 Timothy 2:15-26

GET STARTED
Lesson 5. What if Everyone's Doing It?

GRAPPLE SCHEDULE

5 MINUTES	HANG TIME
10 MINUTES	GRAPPLE CHAT
10-15 MINUTES	GRAPPLE TIME
20-25 MINUTES	TEAM TIME
10 MINUTES	TEAM REPORTS
5 MINUTES	PRAYER & CHALLENGE

SUPPLIES
Bibles, Grapple DVD, DVD player, music CD, CD player, copy of the Grapple Team Guide for each person, paper, pens or pencils, 3x5 cards or slips of paper (two per student), markers, small pieces of masking tape

BIBLE BASIS FOR TEACHERS
The Passage: 2 Timothy 2:15-26
Scholars believe 2 Timothy was the last letter Paul wrote before his death. Timothy was a young pastor, and Paul was writing to encourage Timothy to stand firm in his faith. In this passage, Paul specifically warned Timothy about false teachings and encouraged him to remain on the path of truth. Paul also told Timothy to avoid temptation and keep himself pure and honorable. Because his age perhaps made him more easily influenced, Timothy was in danger of falling victim to pressure from peers as well as other temptations from his culture. Paul wanted to affirm Timothy and his pursuit of the truth and, at the same time, warn him of the dangers and temptations that surrounded him at all times.

How does this relate to the Grapple Question? Junior highers today are constantly faced with the influence of peer pressure. If "everyone" is doing something, no matter what it is, many people conclude that the dangers involved are minimal. Even if a junior higher perceives the dangers involved in certain activities, the desire to be accepted is often far greater than the desire to avoid danger. All people, not just teenagers, want to be accepted and to take part in meaningful relationships. It's understandable why teenagers give in to the pressure to do what everyone else is doing. For this lesson, students will grapple with this conflict of interest: Do I do what everyone else is doing, or do I honor God and risk not being accepted?

How does this connect to Jesus? Jesus was the quintessential non-conformist. He didn't cave under pressure or try to follow the crowd. When we commit to living a life for Jesus, we are called to follow him instead of the crowd. Honoring God in the name of Jesus may be difficult at times, especially when our friends are trying to convince us to do the opposite. Maybe that's part of what Jesus meant when he said, *"If any of you wants to be my follower, you must turn from your selfish ways, take up your cross, and follow me"* (Mark 8:34).

GRAPPLE HANG TIME: 5 MINUTES
Play music as kids enjoy snacks and friendship, and then play an opening countdown from the Grapple DVD to wrap up Grapple Hang Time.

GRAPPLE CHAT: 10 MINUTES
Have students form pairs; if you have an uneven number of kids, it's OK to have one trio in the mix. Ask each group to chat about two of the four topics below that relate to today's grapple topic. (Answers in parentheses are samples.)

IN PAIRS
Chat 1: Find out what everyone asked Aaron to do while Moses was on the mountain with God. (Make gods, Exodus 32:1-8)

Chat 2: Can you do a handstand? How did you learn to do this?

Chat 3: Find out what Jesus says to do with your light, and then put his instructions in your own words. (Let your light shine so that others will praise God, Matthew 5:14-16)

Chat 4: How many things have you done every day this last week?

GRAPPLE TIME: 10-15 MINUTES
Get Ready: Cue the Grapple DVD to the "Everyone's Doin' It" clip, and be prepared to distribute 3x5 cards (or slips of paper) and pens or pencils.

Lead the entire class in the following:

I'm giving each of you two 3x5 cards (or slips of paper) and a pen (or pencil). On one card, write something teenagers really like to do; on the other write something that's right to do. Write something different on each card, even though the categories might overlap. When students have finished, collect cards and pens. Shuffle all the cards together; you don't need to keep the like-to-do cards separate from the right-to-do ones.

Find a partner. I'll read two of these cards, and then share with your partner which one you'd rather do and why. Ready? Read two cards, and allow a minute for discussion. Continue by asking students to find new partners and reading another pair of options until you've run out of options. If you have additional time, you can reshuffle and continue reading.

IN PAIRS
How do most people determine what's right, and what's not right, to do in life? How do you determine what's right and what's not right to do?

TELL ALL
When have you had to choose between what you wanted to do and what you knew you should do? Explain. Without naming anyone, what have you seen teenagers do just to gain others' acceptance? What did they sacrifice and/or gain? What's the limit, the line beyond which you shouldn't go in order to gain someone else's acceptance?

Show the "Everyone's Doin' It" clip on the Grapple DVD.

Today we're discussing one of life's biggest dilemmas: How do I choose between what I know is right and what others are doing? Will others still like me if I choose what's right and refuse to do what they want? Will I still like myself if I go with the flow? Do my choices even matter? And how do I know what's right anyway? What if everyone's doing it? Let's grapple with that!

GRAPPLE TEAM TIME: 20-25 MINUTES
Break into Grapple Teams. Encourage Grapple Team leaders to check in with kids about their week. Grapple Team leaders will facilitate discussion, using the Grapple Team Guide on pages 47-48. Afterward, students will report what they learned.

GRAPPLE TEAM REPORTS: 10 MINUTES
At the end of Grapple Team Time, match Grapple Teams that chose Option 1 with Grapple Teams that chose Option 2 from page 48. Have teams present their reports.

(If you have an uneven number of teams, simply form one group of three teams for the presentations. If you have only two Grapple Teams, simply do the presentations one team at a time.)

GRAPPLE PRAYER AND CHALLENGE: 5 MINUTES
Read the Grapple Prayer options. Have the class choose one prayer option that everyone will do. Allow students time to pray about what they discovered. Then close in prayer.

Get Ready: For Option 1, distribute markers and small pieces of masking tape.

Option 1: Sticky Situations

Write one of your weaknesses on a small piece of masking tape. Put the tape on your arm, leg, or face. Then pray, asking God to be strong in your weakness. Ask God to speak up for you as your enemy tries to hurt you.

Option 2: Power Prayers

Clench your fists tight as you imagine using all your power to maintain control over all the different areas of your life. Talk with God, asking for his powerful perspective, and gradually unclench your fists as you give God control. With your hands open and empty, ask God to fill you with his empowering, life-giving Spirit.

GRAPPLE CHALLENGE

If everyone's doing it, why shouldn't I? Everyone struggles with this—even your parents and teachers still struggle from time to time to do the right thing instead of the popular thing. You've heard lots of good advice on things you should and shouldn't do, but none of that really matters until you make the choice to follow Jesus in your actions and attitudes. Then God will give you the strength to make the right choice, even when it's hard. You can choose to honor God in the way you live. Each time you make a choice, ask yourself whether or not it's a decision that will honor God. Pray that God will transform you into a new person, and then act accordingly.

WEEKLY GRAPPLE CONNECTION

Grapple Question: What if Everyone's Doing It?
Kids Learn: I Will Honor God
Dig Into the Bible: 2 Timothy 2:15-26

Peer pressure. It's something every kid has to deal with, and the idea makes parents everywhere cringe. Even the best-behaved teenager can be swayed by the crowd.

But peer pressure affects adults, too. Have you encountered a situation recently in which you were torn between following someone else and standing alone for something you felt was right? Maybe your boss wanted you to fudge a few numbers, or a friend asked you to tell a "little white lie." This week, share with your teenager how you felt about these experiences—it can help your teenager come to you the next time he or she faces a sticky situation.

GRAPPLE TEAM GUIDE LESSON 5

In your Grapple Team, use this guide to grapple with today's question.

Stand facing a partner. Press your palms against your partner's palms. Push hard and count to 30.

IN PAIRS

How is peer pressure like the pressure you just felt? Share a time you chose to do something that went against the popular current and how you handled it. Can you think of a situation in which it's OK for someone else to do something that's not OK for you to do? Explain.

We call ourselves Christians because we follow Christ's example. Let's take a look at two accounts of things Jesus did.

Read Matthew 13:53-58 and Mark 3:1-6

What did Jesus do in these passages? What else could Jesus have done? How did people respond to Jesus' actions?

_____

_____

_____

IN PAIRS

If you had been there, how do you think you would have reacted to Jesus' actions? Why would Jesus purposely choose to anger people?

The Apostle Paul gave his friend Timothy some advice about how to follow Jesus.

Read 2 Timothy 2:15-26

Fold a piece of paper to make three columns, and then label them as follows: "Do," "Don't," and "So What?" In the "Do" column, write what Paul told Timothy to do. In the "Don't" column, write what Paul told Timothy not to do. In the "So what?" column write why Paul advised Timothy to do or not do these things.

Read some more of Paul's instructions for living.

Read Colossians 3:1-15

Add anything new/different to your columns. What does Paul mean when he says you "died to this life"? How would following Paul's instructions impact your life, specifically? What benefits or risks would you encounter by living this way?

_____

_____

_____

IN PAIRS

On a scale of 1 to 5, how closely does your life reflect Paul's advice? Explain. What price have you paid and are you now paying to follow Christ?

Read Romans 12:1-2

According to this passage, where does the power to live differently come from? How can you follow Paul's advice? How easy/difficult would that be to do?

_____

_____

_____

GRAPPLE TEAM REPORTS

With your team, choose one of the options below to report what you discovered.

Option 1: Knowit Poets!
Write a poem or a rap about what you learned today, making every sentence contain the word choice.

Option 2: New Perspective
Talk about how today's lesson has changed your perspective on peer pressure. And then get a new physical perspective: Stand on a table, stand on your head, stretch out on the floor—whatever you want! Hold that position as one member of your team explains how today's lesson has provided a new perspective. Do a "test run" as a team before making your presentation to the other team.

WHAT IF EVERYONE'S DOING IT?
(STUDENT)

2 Timothy 2:21
If you keep yourself pure, you will be a special utensil for honorable use. Your life will be clean, and you will be ready for the Master to use you for every good work.

GRAPPLE CHAT
Chat 1: Find out what everyone asked Aaron to do while Moses was on the mountain with God.

Chat 2: Can you do a handstand? How did you learn to do this?

Chat 3: Find out what Jesus says to do with your light, and then put his instructions in your own words.

Chat 4: How many things have you done every day this last week?

GRAPPLE CHALLENGE
Every time you make a choice this week, consider carefully whether or not it would honor God, and then choose only that which would honor God.

NOTES:

_____

_____

_____

_____

_____

_____

_____

_____

TO DO OR NOT TO DO?

CAN I *REALLY* HEAR GOD?

TO DO OR NOT TO DO?

Can I *Really* Hear God?
The Point: I Will Listen to God
The Passages: Deuteronomy 6:4-5; 1 Kings 19:9-18; Psalm 1:1-2; 34:11;
Luke 10:25-28; John 10:27-30; 14:8-11; James 1:22-25; 1 John 4:1-6

GET STARTED
Lesson 6. Can I *Really* Hear God?

GRAPPLE SCHEDULE

5 MINUTES	HANG TIME
10 MINUTES	GRAPPLE CHAT
10-15 MINUTES	GRAPPLE TIME
20-25 MINUTES	TEAM TIME
10 MINUTES	TEAM REPORTS
5 MINUTES	PRAYER & CHALLENGE

SUPPLIES
Bibles, Grapple DVD, DVD player, music CD, CD player, copy of the Grapple
Team Guide for each person, paper, pens or pencils

BIBLE BASIS FOR TEACHERS
The Passage: 1 Kings 19:9-18
When Ahab told Jezebel what had happened to the false prophets on Mount
Carmel, she was furious and vowed to kill Elijah within 24 hours. Even though
Ahab had witnessed God's power on the mountain, he apparently did nothing to
oppose Jezebel. Elijah ran for his life.

Elijah's fear of Jezebel may seem out of character for a prophet of God, but
remember that no human is perfect. After the events on Mount Carmel, Elijah
may have been physically and emotionally exhausted. Maybe he tired of the fight.
Or perhaps he was disappointed that his life was still in danger. Maybe he was
overwhelmed by the prospect of another spiritual battle. Whatever the reason, he
felt he'd had enough and retreated into the wilderness. Even though Elijah's faith
was apparently weak at this point, God was faithful and brought food and drink
to him. Then, after eating and drinking, Elijah began a 40-day journey to Mount
Sinai, the mountain of God. He was seeking some assurance that God was still
with him.

How does this relate to the Grapple Question? Elijah's statement in 1 Kings
19:10 reveals his feelings. He felt alone, abandoned by the Israelites, and tired of
running and hiding to protect his life. It seemed to him that he was the only one in
the world who truly followed God. He may have even doubted God's protection,

providence, and presence. Sometimes we feel the same way. We wonder where God is and why God is so silent. Elijah shared his feelings with God, and God—in the aftermath of a windstorm, an earthquake, and a fire—responded in a whisper. If Elijah hadn't been listening carefully, he would have missed God's voice. The same is true for us. We need to be listening attentively to hear God whispering to us.

How does this connect to Jesus? Jesus would frequently retreat from his day-to-day ministries in order to pray and listen to God (Matthew 14:23). Like Jesus, we get involved in the messiness of life. We often become overwhelmed by the noise and chaos all around us. Sometimes we need to take Jesus' example to heart and retreat in order to hear God speaking to us. God is speaking to us; we just need to escape the busyness—the "windstorms," "earthquakes," and "fires" that consume our daily lives—and listen.

GRAPPLE HANG TIME: 5 MINUTES
Play music as kids enjoy snacks and friendship, and then play an opening countdown from the Grapple DVD to wrap up Grapple Hang Time.

GRAPPLE CHAT: 10 MINUTES
Have students form pairs; if you have an uneven number of kids, it's OK to have one trio in the mix. Ask each group to chat about two of the four topics below that relate to today's grapple topic. (Answers in parentheses are samples.)

IN PAIRS
Chat 1: Find the name of a child God woke from his sleep. (Samuel, 1 Samuel 3:1-10)

Chat 2: How far away does your farthest friend or relative live? How often do you get to see this person?

Chat 3: Discover what King Josiah did when Hilkiah brought him the lost Book of the Law. (King Josiah tore his clothes, 2 Kings 22:11)

Chat 4: What's your personal record for your longest phone conversation?

GRAPPLE TIME: 10-15 MINUTES
Get Ready: Prepare to play music on your CD player—the volume will matter more than the style of music on your CD. Cue the Grapple DVD to the "Listening for God" clip.

Lead the entire class in the following:

Find a partner, and stand on opposite sides of the room. I want you to have a conversation about what you did this past weekend or what you plan to do this next weekend. As you talk, I'm going to begin playing some music. See if you can still have your conversation.

Begin by playing the music quietly; then slowly turn up the volume to the point where students either cannot hear or struggle to hear each other's words.

TELL ALL
Was this activity fun or frustrating? Why? What challenges did you face? What would have made this task easier? When was the last time you had to listen really hard to someone? How would you define the word listen *to someone who didn't know what it meant?*

IN PAIRS
What are some of your favorite sounds? What's a sound you wish you could hear but haven't?

Show the "Listening for God" clip on the Grapple DVD.

We listen for entertainment, information, and understanding. We listen because we can, because we want to, and sometimes because we're told to. But when people tell you to listen, they often expect you to do something in response to what they said. God wants us to listen, too, but what does that mean? How can we listen to God? What does God's voice sound like? How does God communicate? Can we really hear God? Let's grapple with that!

GRAPPLE TEAM TIME: 20-25 MINUTES
Break into Grapple Teams. Encourage Grapple Team leaders to check in with kids about their week. Grapple Team leaders will facilitate discussion, using the Grapple Team Guide on pages 57-58. Afterward, students will report what they learned.

GRAPPLE TEAM REPORTS: 10 MINUTES
At the end of Grapple Team Time, match Grapple Teams that chose Option 1 with Grapple Teams that chose Option 2 from page 58. Have teams present their reports.

(If you have an uneven number of teams, simply form one group of three teams for the presentations. If you have only two Grapple Teams, simply do the presentations one team at a time.)

GRAPPLE PRAYER AND CHALLENGE: 5 MINUTES
Read the Grapple Prayer options. Have the class choose one prayer option that everyone will do. Allow students time to pray about what they discovered. Then close in prayer.

Get Ready: For Option 1, make sure students have paper and pens or pencils.

Option 1: Prayer Pile
Get in a circle with the rest of your group. Write a prayer to God. Then crumple up the paper with the prayer on it and make a pile of crumpled papers in the middle

of the circle. Choose one crumpled prayer from the pile. Silently pray the words written on the paper, and then ask God to answer the prayer for the person who wrote it.

Option 2: Little and Big

Think of "little" sins from this past week that you might have thought were too insignificant to confess. Confess these to God, and ask God to help you change your attitude about all sin—even the "little" sins.

GRAPPLE CHALLENGE

Has anyone ever accused you of "selective listening"? That means you choose to hear only the things you want to hear and tune out the things you don't want to hear. Usually parents or teachers describe this as a negative thing. For example, a parent or teacher might say you didn't hear about that homework assignment because you tuned out the wrong person at the wrong time. Well, this week I challenge you to use selective listening in a good way by tuning your ear to hear God's voice. Spend time loving God as you read the Bible, pray, and talk with others who will help you hear God and know what God wants you to do. The more you listen, the more you'll be amazed at how much God wants to speak to you.

WEEKLY GRAPPLE CONNECTION

Grapple Question: Can I Really Hear God?
Kids Learn: I Will Listen to God
Dig Into the Bible: 1 Kings 19:9-18

Does your teenager suffer from a case of selective listening—choosing to hear only the things he or she wants to hear and "tuning out" the other things? For instance, your child "conveniently" didn't hear your request to wash the car but was all ears when you gave permission to go to a friend's house.

Does God also feel that way—we hear God rewarding and encouraging us, but we don't listen when God is convicting us of something we need to change? God wants us to listen, but what does that mean? Just how do we listen to God? What does God's voice sound like? How does God communicate?

We can learn to hear God speaking to us, but it takes some work. Do something to set an example for your teenager this week. Read the Bible, pray, or talk with others who will help you hear God and know what God wants you to do. The more you listen, the more you'll be amazed at how much God wants to speak to you—and to your child.

GRAPPLE TEAM GUIDE LESSON 6

In your Grapple Team, use this guide to grapple with today's question.

Sit in a circle, close your eyes, and imagine God sitting in front of you. What do you think God might say to your group right now? After a moment, open your eyes, and share it with the group.

IN PAIRS

Do you think God really talks to people? Why or why not? How would you know if God were speaking to you? Do you think you've ever heard from God? If so, share your experience.

Read 1 Kings 19:9-18

Draw five scenes to show what happened in this story.

What about this story surprises you? If you had been Elijah, in which scene would you have expected to hear God? What can you learn about hearing God from Elijah's experience?

_____

_____

_____

Read John 14:8-11 and John 10:27-30

In your own words, what was Jesus' relationship with God the Father like? What does he say about hearing God? Do you think it's possible to be one with God the way Jesus was? Why or why not? What would that be like?

_____

_____

_____

IN PAIRS

After reading these verses, how do you think God might speak to people today? Would you like to hear God speak to you? Why or why not?

Read Deuteronomy 6:4-5 and Luke 10:25-28

What does love have to do with hearing from God? Do you have to feel love to act lovingly? What's the difference?

_____

_____

_____

On a separate sheet of paper, draw a picture of at least one way you can express love for God. On the other side, draw another picture of at least one way God expresses his love for you.

Read Psalm 1:1-2; 34:11; James 1:22-25; and 1 John 4:1-6

IN PAIRS

What do these passages say about how you can listen to God? What would listening to God in this way look like in your life? What could you do this week to apply these passages to your life?

GRAPPLE TEAM REPORTS

With your team, choose one of the options below to report what you discovered.

Option 1: Top 5

Create a Top 5 list of the most important, challenging, or meaningful things you learned today. Be prepared to explain why each item on the list is so important, challenging, or meaningful.

Option 2: Movie Illustration

Together, think of a scene from a movie that illustrates what you learned today. Be prepared to describe that scene and explain why it illustrates what you've learned.

CAN I REALLY HEAR GOD?

(STUDENT)

2 Timothy 2:21

If you keep yourself pure, you will be a special utensil for honorable use. Your life will be clean, and you will be ready for the Master to use you for every good work.

GRAPPLE CHAT

Chat 1: Find the name of a child God woke from his sleep.

Chat 2: How far away does your farthest friend or relative live? How often do you get to see this person?

Chat 3: Discover what King Josiah did when Hilkiah brought him the lost Book of the Law.

Chat 4: What's your personal record for your longest phone conversation?

GRAPPLE CHALLENGE

When you're reading the Bible, praying, or talking to people this week, be extra attentive for God's voice—God may have something to say to you.

NOTES:

_____

_____

_____

_____

_____

_____

_____

_____

TO DO OR NOT TO DO?

ISN'T IT *MY* MONEY?

TO DO OR NOT TO DO?

Isn't It *My* Money?
The Point: I Will Care About Financial Stewardship
The Passages: Proverbs 22:1-16; Matthew 6:19-33; 1 Timothy 6:6-10, 17-19; 1 John 3:16-17

GET STARTED
Lesson 7. Isn't It *My* Money?

GRAPPLE SCHEDULE

5 MINUTES	HANG TIME
10 MINUTES	GRAPPLE CHAT
10-15 MINUTES	GRAPPLE TIME
20-25 MINUTES	TEAM TIME
10 MINUTES	TEAM REPORTS
5 MINUTES	PRAYER & CHALLENGE

SUPPLIES
Bibles, Grapple DVD, DVD player, music CD, CD player, copy of the Grapple Team Guide for each person, paper, pens or pencils, 3x5 cards or slips of paper, copies of maps printed from a mapping website, modeling dough or clay

BIBLE BASIS FOR TEACHERS
The Passage: Proverbs 22:1-16
These verses come from a collection of sayings attributed to King Solomon, many of which speak to how we ought to regard wealth. Solomon articulated several truths in these proverbs: Reputation is more important than money, God created everyone, wealth does not make one person "more equal" than another, financial gain is not an end in itself, money can enslave a person, and it is good to be generous toward the poor. Solomon framed his proverbs on wealth around "humility and fear of the Lord." By way of contrast, the other proverbs in this passage warn against injustice, laziness, immorality, and foolishness—it's easy to see how these attitudes pertain to money as well. Solomon counseled that a person who follows such a "treacherous road" will "end in poverty."

How does this relate to the Grapple Question? People today sometimes believe that they are entitled to certain things: a roof over their heads, food on the table, two cars in the garage, and money in the bank. Not only do people sometimes feel entitled to these things, but they conclude that they can do what they please with them. Junior highers aren't any different. Some may believe that when they receive money or possessions for a birthday, for performing a job, or for getting good grades, they can do whatever they want with it. Isn't it their money? This lesson will help students grapple with the idea of entitlement as well as how they can spend (or save) their money responsibly.

How does this connect to Jesus? Jesus understood people. He knew that people are tempted by wealth and are often consumed with obtaining more and more money and possessions. Jesus said, *"No one can serve two masters. For you will hate one and love the other; you will be devoted to one and despise the other. You cannot serve both God and money" (Matthew 6:24).* Jesus didn't hate money, and he didn't suggest that we do away with it. We need money to survive, and Jesus knew that. Jesus warned against allowing the lust for money to control our actions. Jesus and Solomon both counseled that when we are humble, generous, and responsible with our money, we remain loyal to God as the master of our life. We can control our money rather than be controlled by it.

GRAPPLE HANG TIME: 5 MINUTES
Play music as kids enjoy snacks and friendship, and then play an opening countdown from the Grapple DVD to wrap up Grapple Hang Time.

GRAPPLE CHAT: 10 MINUTES
Have students form pairs; if you have an uneven number of kids, it's OK to have one trio in the mix. Ask each group to chat about two of the four topics below that relate to today's grapple topic. (Answers in parentheses are samples.)

IN PAIRS
Chat 1: Find out what Jacob vowed to give God after his dream at Bethel. (In return for God's presence and protection, Jacob vowed to give God one-tenth of all God gave him, Genesis 28:10-22)

Chat 2: What's a recent example of a "reward for a job well done" you've received?

Chat 3: Discover who the tax collector from Jericho was and what he did after he met Jesus. (Zacchaeus gave half his wealth to the poor and paid back those he had cheated four times what he had taken from them, Luke 19:1-10)

Chat 4: What's the most amount of money you've seen in one place?

GRAPPLE TIME: 10-15 MINUTES
Get Ready: Cue the Grapple DVD to the "It's My Money" clip, and be prepared to distribute a 3x5 card (or a slip of paper) and a pen or pencil to each student.

Lead the entire class in the following:

I'm handing you a 3x5 card (or slip of paper) and a pen (or pencil). A distant relative has given you $2,000. The money is yours to do with as you please, but if you use it all to help other people, you'll receive an extra $2,000 to spend helping *them—a total of $4,000. But if you use the money only for yourself, you get only $2,000. On one side of the card, write down what you'd do with the money.*

Now, let me give you a different scenario. You've worked really hard all summer and earned $2,000. You are free to spend your earnings however you wish. On the other side of the card, write down what you'd do with this $2,000.

TELL ALL
What did you do with the money given to you by your relative, and why? What did you do with the money you earned? Why? Explain the differences between your answers to the two scenarios, if there were any.

IN PAIRS
Describe a time when someone told you what to do with money you worked hard to earn. How does it make you feel when someone tells you what to do with your money?

TELL ALL
What are some things that we absolutely deserve? How does it make you feel when you don't get recognized for your hard work? Describe a time when you received something you didn't deserve. Why do you think "deserving" attitudes sometimes cause problems?

Let's watch a clip.

Show the "It's My Money" clip on the Grapple DVD.

If you work really hard on a school project, you probably deserve a good grade. If your team trains hard and plays well, you may deserve to win. And if you do your best job at work, you might deserve a raise. But do you deserve a bazillion bucks? And even if you do earn a lot of money, do you deserve to spend it however you please? After all, isn't it your money? Let's grapple with that!

GRAPPLE TEAM TIME: 20-25 MINUTES
Break into Grapple Teams. Encourage Grapple Team leaders to check in with kids about their week. Grapple Team leaders will facilitate discussion, using the Grapple Team Guide on pages 67-68. Afterward, students will report what they learned.

GRAPPLE TEAM REPORTS: 10 MINUTES
At the end of Grapple Team Time, match Grapple Teams that chose Option 1 with Grapple Teams that chose Option 2 from page 68. Have teams present their reports.

(If you have an uneven number of teams, simply form one group of three teams for the presentations. If you have only two Grapple Teams, simply do the presentations one team at a time.)

GRAPPLE PRAYER AND CHALLENGE: 5 MINUTES

Read the Grapple Prayer options. Have the class choose one prayer option that everyone will do. Allow students time to pray about what they discovered. Then close in prayer.

Get Ready: For Option 1, distribute copies of maps printed from a mapping website.

Option 1: Roadmap of Wisdom

Look at a map, and consider all the different roads and highways and streets featured on that map. Pray for God's guidance, wisdom, and direction in your life, and ask God for strength in following the path and plan he has created for you.

Option 2: Still Small Voice

Close your eyes and think about one difficult thing you're currently going through. Ask God to show you where he is in this situation. After a period of reflective silence, ask God what he is trying to say to you through this circumstance. Write down any thoughts or ideas that come to mind.

GRAPPLE CHALLENGE

How we handle money says a lot about how we view God. Do we really believe that all good gifts come from God and that God will provide for us? If so, we can be wise about money and not allow it to control us. This week, I challenge you: Carry a penny in your pocket at all times. Each time you touch it or any other coin, remember to give thanks for everything God has given you. Turn your "deserving" attitude into gratitude and watch what God does in your heart.

WEEKLY GRAPPLE CONNECTION

Grapple Question: Isn't It My Money?
Kids Learn: I Will Care About Financial Stewardship
Dig Into the Bible: Proverbs 22:1-16

What lessons do your kids learn from watching how you spend money? Would you consider yourself generous, selfish, or somewhere in between? Do they see you making impulsive purchases when you run into the store for just one item? Do they notice you carefully setting aside money for a long-anticipated vacation? Do they observe you tithing at church or donating to charities?

Give some thought to this question: What values about finances do you want your son or daughter to learn from you? Maybe you want to instill the value of living within your means, staying out of debt, or tithing faithfully. Now seriously consider whether your current lifestyle supports those values. Put those goals in writing, show your goals to your teenager, and review them every month to make sure you are staying on track. You can make a difference in your teenager's attitude about money.

GRAPPLE TEAM GUIDE LESSON 7

In your Grapple Team, use this guide to grapple with today's question.

Share with your group: If you had all the money you could want, what three things would you do with it, and why?

IN PAIRS

What's the most money you've ever had? What did you do with it? How did you decide what to do with it?

Read Proverbs 22:1-16

Based on your first impression, what does this passage say about money? Read it again and, on a separate sheet of paper, put into your own words each verse that directly or indirectly has to do with money and/or people's attitudes and actions regarding money.

_____

_____

_____

What do you think the writer of Proverbs would suggest is the "right path" concerning money? What do these verses have to do with you?

_____

_____

_____

Turn your paper over and make two columns, labeled "Money/Stuff" and "God." Using Proverbs 22:1-16 as a reference, write down what money and possessions provide in the "Money/Stuff" column and write down what God provides in the "God" column.

IN PAIRS

How have you seen money affect people's attitudes? their behavior? their relationships? How could you use money wisely to improve your attitudes and relationships?

Read Matthew 6:19-33

Add to the columns what Jesus tells his followers about money and God. Why can't you serve both? Why does money have such a powerful influence over us? What do these verses have to say about the ways people use money—spending, saving, giving, and so on?

_____

_____

_____

IN PAIRS

What do you treasure in your life? What do you think that says about your heart?

Read 1 Timothy 6:6-10, 17-19 and 1 John 3:16-17

Again, add what you read here to the "Money/Stuff" and "God" columns. According to these passages, how would you explain contentment? What do these verses have to say about the ways people use money, such as spending, saving, giving, and so on?

_____

_____

_____

IN PAIRS

How would you sum up what you've learned today? Is it bad to have or want money? Why or why not?

GRAPPLE TEAM REPORTS

With your team, choose one of the options below to report what you discovered.

Get Ready: For Option 2, distribute modeling dough or clay.

Option 1: Relay Report

Discuss some of the big ideas you've learned today. Once you're ready to make your presentation to the other team, line up on one side of the room. Run down to the other end of the room and back. When you return, tell about something you learned today. Then the next person in line runs to the end of the room and back, and reports something else. Continue until everyone has participated.

Option 2: Sculpt It

Take some modeling dough or clay, and sculpt objects that explain or reveal what you discovered today.

ISN'T IT MY MONEY?
(STUDENT)

2 Timothy 2:21
If you keep yourself pure, you will be a special utensil for honorable use. Your life will be clean, and you will be ready for the Master to use you for every good work.

GRAPPLE CHAT
Chat 1: Find out what Jacob vowed to give God after his dream at Bethel.

Chat 2: What's a recent example of a "reward for a job well done" you've received?

Chat 3: Discover who the tax collector from Jericho was and what he did after he met Jesus.

Chat 4: What's the most amount of money you've seen in one place?

GRAPPLE CHALLENGE
Carry a penny in your pocket this week, and every time you touch it—or any other coin—offer thanks for everything God has given you.

NOTES:
_____

_____

_____

_____

_____

_____

_____

_____

TO DO OR NOT TO DO?

CAN'T I JUST WATCH TV?

TO DO OR NOT TO DO?

Can't I Just Watch TV?
The Point: I Will Use My Gifts and Talents
The Passages: Matthew 14:22-33; 25:14-30; 1 Corinthians 12:14-21;
2 Timothy 1:6-7; 1 Peter 4:10-11

GET STARTED
Lesson 8. Can't I Just Watch TV?

GRAPPLE SCHEDULE

5 MINUTES	HANG TIME
10 MINUTES	GRAPPLE CHAT
10-15 MINUTES	GRAPPLE TIME
20-25 MINUTES	TEAM TIME
10 MINUTES	TEAM REPORTS
5 MINUTES	PRAYER & CHALLENGE

SUPPLIES
Bibles, Grapple DVD, DVD player, music CD, CD player, copy of the Grapple Team Guide for each person, paper, pens or pencils

BIBLE BASIS FOR TEACHERS
The Passage: Matthew 25:14-30
A few days before Jesus was betrayed and arrested, he took his disciples to the Mount of Olives and taught them to prepare for the End Times. Jesus told them about signs that would precede the end, ways to be prepared, and what the final judgment would be like. In the parable of the three servants, Jesus gave the disciples, and every other Christian, advice about how to live—always anticipating Jesus' return. In this particular parable, Jesus told about a master who was going away on a long trip. Before leaving, the master entrusted his three servants with different amounts of money. The first servant received five bags of silver and earned five more. The second servant received two bags of silver and earned two more. The third servant received one bag of silver and buried it in the ground because he was afraid of his master. The master commended the first two servants for being wise and faithful stewards. However, he condemned and punished the third servant for being wicked and lazy. The parable concludes with a promise and a warning. Those who use what God has given them will be given more. Those who do nothing will lose even what little they have.

How does this relate to the Grapple Question? God has blessed everyone with talents, gifts, and skills. Some people seem to have an abundance of these, while others feel that they have only one thing they can do well. Whatever the case may be, God wants us to use and develop our gifts and talents in order to bless the world. Whether we've been gifted with a great singing voice, the ability to write creatively, or the ability to run fast, how can we bless others with the talents and gifts God has given us? Often, it's tempting for teenagers to sit on the couch all day, watch movies, or play video games. When does hanging out and relaxing with friends become laziness? At what point are we held accountable for using, or not using, the gifts we've been given?

How does this connect to Jesus? On the surface, it doesn't seem like the third servant in this parable did anything to deserve the punishment he received. He didn't spend the money and lose it—he just saved it. Upon further examination, Jesus was pretty clear in this story. Jesus was teaching that it is better to try and fail than to never try at all. God wants us to use the gifts and talents he's given us to serve the world. Sometimes we neglect to use our gifts because we're afraid, we're lazy, or we just want to procrastinate. In the end, God will hold us accountable.

GRAPPLE HANG TIME: 5 MINUTES
Play music as kids enjoy snacks and friendship, and then play an opening countdown from the Grapple DVD to wrap up Grapple Hang Time.

GRAPPLE CHAT: 10 MINUTES
Have students form pairs; if you have an uneven number of kids, it's OK to have one trio in the mix. Ask each group to chat about two of the four topics below that relate to today's grapple topic. (Answers in parentheses are samples.)

IN PAIRS
Chat 1: Find out what gift the Queen of Sheba gave to King Solomon when she dropped in for a visit. (Gift of 9,000 pounds of gold, great quantities of spices, and precious jewels, 1 Kings 10:10)

Chat 2: What's the best gift you've recently given a friend for a birthday, and why was it such a great gift?

Chat 3: Find out what gift Jesus promises to give tired people who come to him. (Rest, Matthew 11:28-30)

Chat 4: What are your three favorite TV shows, and why?

GRAPPLE TIME: 10-15 MINUTES
Get Ready: Cue the Grapple DVD to the "Use It!" clip.

Lead the entire class in the following:

Get in a big circle. Imagine the wildest thing you would do—your biggest, craziest dream—if you knew there was no way you could fail. Pause. Now think of a body posture that represents what you would do. Pause. On the count of three, assume that posture, and then hold it while we go around and see what everyone would do. Ready? One, two, three: pose!

While students are posed, move around the circle interviewing kids about what they'd do and—if necessary—how the poses represent the activities. Have fun with this!

IN PAIRS
Do you think you'll ever fulfill your dream? Why or why not? What other dreams did you hear that you'd like to go for? Which ones seem unrealistic, and why?

TELL ALL
Raise your hand if you think you'll ever attempt to live out your dream. Look around: Does it surprise you that so many/few think they'll follow through on their dreams? How powerful is the fear of failure at this time in your life? Are you as afraid of failure as your best friends are? Why or why not? How does fear of failure influence what you'll try? Who or what influences you?

IN PAIRS
When have you tried something new and failed? Were you able to enjoy it despite the failure? Did you keep at it, or give up? How did that experience affect your willingness to keep trying new things?

Show the "Use It!" clip on the Grapple DVD.

How do you know if you're good at something unless you try? Actually, most people who are truly good at something probably failed a few times along the way. Practice makes perfect, right? But with so much pressure to perform and so many people who might be better than you, why even try? Give up, or go for it? Can't we just sit around and watch TV instead of trying something new? Let's grapple with that!

GRAPPLE TEAM TIME: 20-25 MINUTES
Break into Grapple Teams. Encourage Grapple Team leaders to check in with kids about their week. Grapple Team leaders will facilitate discussion, using the Grapple Team Guide on pages 77-79. Afterward, students will report what they learned.

GRAPPLE TEAM REPORTS: 10 MINUTES
At the end of Grapple Team Time, match Grapple Teams that chose Option 1 with Grapple Teams that chose Option 2 from page 79. Have teams present their reports.

(If you have an uneven number of teams, simply form one group of three teams for the presentations. If you have only two Grapple Teams, simply do the presentations one team at a time.)

GRAPPLE PRAYER AND CHALLENGE: 5 MINUTES

Read the Grapple Prayer options. Have the class choose one prayer option that everyone will do. Allow students time to pray about what they discovered. Then close in prayer.

Option 1: Letter Prayers

Write a letter to Jesus. Tell him what you know is true about him and what you're unsure about; ask for his strength and help in developing a deeper trust in him.

Option 2: Power Prayers

Clench your fists tight as you imagine using all your power to maintain control over all the different areas of your life. Talk with God, asking for his powerful perspective, and gradually unclench your fists as you give God control. With your hands open and empty, ask God to fill you with his empowering, life-giving Spirit.

GRAPPLE CHALLENGE

Have you ever thought that the desire to try something new might come from God? Whether you really want to try out for the swim team or dream of going on a short-term mission trip, there's a good chance it's because that's where God wants you. Don't give up! Go for it! When you find yourself paralyzed by fear, or comparing yourself to others, or dismissing some new dream, or tempted to give up, stop, pray, and go for it. I bet you'll find Jesus there, holding out his hand, asking you to have faith and keep walking.

WEEKLY GRAPPLE CONNECTION

Grapple Question: Can't I Just Watch TV?
Kids Learn: I Will Use My Gifts and Talents
Dig Into the Bible: Matthew 25:14-30

Does it seem like all your teenager wants to do is sit in front of the TV or computer all day? Is it like pulling teeth to get him or her to stop texting and do something more constructive? What about those gifts and talents God has given your child—how can you encourage your teenager to try something new?

Here's what we're told in 1 Peter 4:10: "God has given each of you a gift from his great variety of spiritual gifts. Use them well to serve one another." In addition to spiritual gifts, God has also blessed your child with talents and skills. Help your teenager identify his or her gifts and skills and use them to serve others. If your teenager likes to cook and has the gift of hospitality, he or she might find joy in cooking for someone who has a new baby or who has recently experienced a death in the family. If your teenager is athletic and has the gift of serving, he or she might find it fulfilling to help a family in your church move to a new home or finish some yard work. Encourage your child to get off the couch and discover his or her talents, skills, and spiritual gifts!

GRAPPLE TEAM GUIDE LESSON 8

In your Grapple Team, use this guide to grapple with today's question.

If there were a new TV show about the kingdom of heaven, what would it be like, and what would people be doing there? Share with your team.

Let's hear one of Jesus' stories describing the kingdom of heaven.

Read Matthew 25:14-15

Before you finish the story, what do you notice about the man's actions? On what "abilities" do you think the man based his decision?

_____

_____

_____

IN PAIRS

What would you do if a man (or God!) handed you a bag of money and asked you to use it to make more money in his absence? What is the "bag of money" God has given you to use—in other words, what valuable things has God given you to grow? How are you growing those gifts right now?

Read Matthew 25:16-18

What do you think of each servant's decision? How do you think their master will respond? What would the servants' options and choices look like if this story took place at your school?

_____

_____

_____

Read Matthew 25:19-30

What do you think of the master's responses to his servants' actions? In your opinion, did the third servant do anything wrong? What could he have done differently? What does this story have to do with your life?

_____

_____

_____

Here comes a totally different illustration...

Read 1 Corinthians 12:14-21

What do you think Paul's point is in this passage? How does this illustration of the body relate to the story of the three servants?

_____

_____

_____

IN PAIRS

In what ways do you compare yourself to others? How does that make you feel about yourself? What does this passage from 1 Corinthians say that can encourage you?

Take a look at Peter living out what he'd learned from Jesus.

Read Matthew 14:22-33

Why did Peter want to walk on water? Why did Jesus let him try? What was Peter feeling when he got back to the boat? What do you think Peter (and the other disciples) learned from this experience? What can you learn from this event?

_____

_____

_____

Read 1 Peter 4:10-11 and 2 Timothy 1:6-7

How might Peter's experience of walking on the water with Jesus have influenced him when he wrote this passage from 1 Peter? What does Peter say about how and why we do things? What's one piece of advice Peter might give you about how you live your life? Based on what you've read, why can't you just watch TV?

GRAPPLE TEAM REPORTS

With your team, choose one of the options below to report what you discovered.

Option 1: Condense It

If you had to summarize today's lesson in only five words, what would they be? As a team, choose the words carefully, and be prepared to explain why you chose them.

Option 2: Project Youth!

With your team, choose your three best ideas about how you could help the youth group learn about today's lesson and put its truths into practice. Be prepared to explain why these truths are important for teenagers to believe and follow.

CAN'T I JUST WATCH TV?
(STUDENT)

2 Timothy 2:21
If you keep yourself pure, you will be a special utensil for honorable use. Your life will be clean, and you will be ready for the Master to use you for every good work.

GRAPPLE CHAT
Chat 1: Find out what gift the Queen of Sheba gave to King Solomon when she dropped in for a visit.

Chat 2: What's the best gift you've recently given a friend for a birthday, and why was it such a great gift?

Chat 3: Find out what gift Jesus promises to give tired people who come to him.

Chat 4: What are your three favorite TV shows, and why?

GRAPPLE CHALLENGE
Whenever you're tempted to sit down and do nothing this week, resist! Practice a gift God has given you.

NOTES:

_____

_____

_____

_____

_____

_____

_____

_____

_____

THE "S" WORD

HOW FAR IS TOO FAR?

THE "S" WORD

How Far Is Too Far?
The Point: I Will Flee From Sexual Immorality
The Passages: Proverbs 4:23; 1 Corinthians 6:12-20; 2 Timothy 2:22

GET STARTED
Lesson 9. How Far Is Too Far?

GRAPPLE SCHEDULE

5 MINUTES	HANG TIME
10 MINUTES	GRAPPLE CHAT
10-15 MINUTES	GRAPPLE TIME
20-25 MINUTES	TEAM TIME
10 MINUTES	TEAM REPORTS
5 MINUTES	PRAYER & CHALLENGE

SUPPLIES
Bibles, Grapple DVD, DVD player, music CD, CD player, copy of the Grapple Team Guide for each person, paper, pens or pencils, 20 pennies for every two students

BIBLE BASIS FOR TEACHERS
The Passage: 1 Corinthians 6:12-20
This passage warns people against sexual sin. Paul provided the church in Corinth with a principle we should follow as Christians. Paul's boundary doesn't encourage us to get as close to the line as we can without crossing over. In fact, the boundary suggests the exact opposite: "Run from sexual sin!" Paul asserts that sexual sin is not only a sin against God and others, but also a sin against our own bodies. Sexual sin dishonors the body, which is "the temple of the Holy Spirit." Jesus Christ purchased our bodies with his own blood on the cross, and when we violate our bodies by sinning sexually, we are dishonoring God.

How does this relate to the Grapple Question? By junior high, kids are being bombarded by hormones. Sex is intriguing, and pushing the limits sexually is tempting. For this lesson, students will grapple with some of these questions: Is making out bad? What if we just kiss with all of our clothes on? Can't we approach the line and get as close to it as possible, as long as we don't cross it? Teenagers begin to rationalize certain behavior as acceptable, while labeling other behavior as taboo. They think that as long as they don't do the taboo behavior, everything will be OK. The Bible has something else to say about sexual behavior. Students will learn that the Bible takes sexual sin very seriously. The Bible advises people not to play with fire and hope to avoid being burned, but to stay away from the fire altogether.

How does this connect to Jesus? First Corinthians 6:15 reads, *"Don't you realize that your bodies are actually parts of Christ?"* When we think about our bodies as parts of Christ, it makes us pause to consider the consequences of treating our bodies badly. If we've devoted our lives to honoring Jesus, why would we do something to our own bodies that would hurt, taint, or destroy part of Jesus? Jesus cares about our lives, including our bodies, and doesn't want us to do anything to hurt ourselves. We don't belong to ourselves—that means our bodies are not ours to do with as we please. We belong to Jesus, who bought us by dying on the cross. So instead of trying to get as close as possible to sex outside of marriage without actually having sex, we should run from sexual sin and honor God with our bodies, as Jesus would have us do.

GRAPPLE HANG TIME: 5 MINUTES
Play music as kids enjoy snacks and friendship, and then play an opening countdown from the Grapple DVD to wrap up Grapple Hang Time.

GRAPPLE CHAT: 10 MINUTES
Have students form pairs; if you have an uneven number of kids, it's OK to have one trio in the mix. Ask each group to chat about two of the four topics below that relate to today's grapple topic. (Answers in parentheses are samples.)

IN PAIRS
Chat 1: Discover and explain how 1+1=1, according to 1 Corinthians. (When two people have sex, they're united, 1 Corinthians 6:16)

Chat 2: Have you ever run a timed race? If so, what was that like?

Chat 3: Find in the Bible what sin you should "run away" from. (Sexual sin, 1 Corinthians 6:18)

Chat 4: How many pairs of shoes do you have, and what are the different purposes of your pairs of shoes?

GRAPPLE TIME: 10-15 MINUTES
Get Ready: Have the class form pairs, and give each pair 20 pennies. Cue the Grapple DVD to the "Choose Your Own Adventure" clip.

Lead the entire class in the following:

It's time to test your ability to hang on to money—literally! Everyone hold one hand in front of you, palm down. Place a penny on the back of your hand. At my signal, flick your hand upward to toss the penny high. Then flip your hand over and catch the penny.

Demonstrate. After everyone has mastered this, ask the person in each pair who's wearing the most blue to stack pennies on the back of his or her hand—as many pennies as the person can catch, but no more.

If you think you can catch three pennies, stop there. Think you can catch eight or nine? Fine. But you must catch all the pennies you toss. Catch them all and you'll get a chance to add to the stack.

Give coin-tossers a second turn if they catch all their pennies. But if pennies are dropped, that person is finished.

Switch partners and repeat. Then collect the pennies.

IN PAIRS

How did you decide how many pennies to try? What happened when you went too far while stacking? When have you pushed something too far and paid the price for it?

TELL ALL

Share the consequences you've paid for pushing the limits.

Let's watch a video that illustrates the concept of pushing the limits.

Show the "Choose Your Own Adventure" clip on the Grapple DVD.

We live in a culture where sex has become invasive. It's challenging sometimes to avoid the explicit sexual undertones, overtones, and in-between tones used by the media and your peers. It's easy to become jaded and think sex just isn't a big deal. Is there a time and place for sex? Doesn't God want us to flee from sexual immorality? What behavior is sexually immoral? How far is too far? Let's grapple with that.

GRAPPLE TEAM TIME: 20-25 MINUTES

Break into Grapple Teams. Encourage Grapple Team leaders to check in with kids about their week. Grapple Team leaders will facilitate discussion, using the Grapple Team Guide on pages 89-90. Afterward, students will report what they learned.

GRAPPLE TEAM REPORTS: 10 MINUTES

At the end of Grapple Team Time, match Grapple Teams that chose Option 1 with Grapple Teams that chose Option 2 from page 90. Have teams present their reports.

(If you have an uneven number of teams, simply form one group of three teams for the presentations. If you have only two Grapple Teams, simply do the presentations one team at a time.)

GRAPPLE PRAYER AND CHALLENGE: 5 MINUTES

Read the Grapple Prayer options. Have the class choose one prayer option that everyone will do. Allow students time to pray about what they discovered. Then close in prayer.

Option 1: Strong Foundation

Stand up, and close your eyes. While balancing on one foot, silently ask God to help you with a challenging situation you're facing right now. Stay in this position as long as you can—up to two minutes, if possible. Then stand on two feet and ask God to help you be a person who will stand confidently in God's strength.

Option 2: Still Small Voice

Close your eyes and think about one difficult thing you're currently going through. Ask God to show you where he is in this situation. After a period of reflective silence, ask God what he is trying to say to you through this circumstance. Write down any thoughts or ideas that come to mind.

GRAPPLE CHALLENGE

I challenge you to let the words of 1 Corinthians speak to you. Now is the time to decide to avoid sexual sin, to draw lines you won't cross later, to do whatever it takes to avoid sexual sin. Decide now how far is too far. Decide now to seek healthy dating relationships, ones that honor God and the person you're with. And decide now that if you feel yourself slipping, you'll turn and leave the situation.

WEEKLY GRAPPLE CONNECTION

Grapple Question: How Far Is Too Far?
Kids Learn: I Will Flee From Sexual Immorality
Dig Into the Bible: 1 Corinthians 6:12-20

I'm sure you've been talking to your teenager about sexual boundaries for a while now. But you know your job's not done. We live in a culture that is increasingly open to loose sexuality, and teenagers are wired to respond somehow. How far can we push the limits before we've gone too far? Is holding hands OK? hugging? kissing? How far is too far? These are some of the dilemmas your teenager struggles with on a daily basis.

If you haven't been talking to your teenager about sexual boundaries, there's no better time than the present. The time for your teenager to make these decisions is not in the heat of the moment—it's now. Talk to your teenager about what a healthy dating relationship looks like. Ask what he or she can do to avoid tempting the opposite sex. Encourage your teenager to decide now to seek healthy dating relationships—ones that honor God and others.

GRAPPLE TEAM GUIDE LESSON 9

In your Grapple Team, use this guide to grapple with today's question.

Two true things about sex:

1. God designed our bodies to enjoy sex. A lot. In the right place and time (marriage), it's dynamite stuff. Powerful. Pure. Positive.

2. God designed our bodies to enjoy sex. In the wrong place and time (outside marriage), sex can be hugely destructive.

The challenge is navigating the in-between time—from now until marriage. How far is too far sexually?

How have your friends answered that question? What do you hear from other people? from the media? Jot their perspectives below:

_____

_____

_____

_____

_____

_____

Share your answers with your team.

Read 1 Corinthians 6:12-20

IN PAIRS

How does the Bible's advice line up with what you wrote? And why run away? Why not stay and—with God's help—wage war against sexual temptations?

Asking "How far can I go?" suggests there's a line where you're safe on this side, unsafe on the other. Do you draw the line at holding hands? kissing? touching above the waist? The problem is, like stacking pennies, you don't know you've pushed past your limit until it's too late to go back.

In your Grapple Team, stand and face a wall—one you can walk to without tripping over anything. Take turns walking briskly to the wall with your eyes closed, hands behind you, leaning forward. How close can you get without breaking your nose? Give it a try, and then continue…

IN PAIRS
If your goal is to avoid breaking your nose, why see how close you can get to the wall? In the same way, if you want to stay sexually pure, why see how far you can go?

Read Proverbs 4:23 and 2 Timothy 2:22

What do these verses suggest about how far to go sexually?

GRAPPLE TEAM REPORTS
With your team, choose one of the options below to report what you discovered.

Option 1: Proverb It
Look through the book of Proverbs and find one verse that best connects to what you learned today. If you have enough time, consider finding additional verses.

Option 2: Instant Object Lesson
Use whatever you can find around you to create some instant object lessons that explain what you learned today. Get creative!

HOW FAR IS TOO FAR?

(STUDENT)

1 Corinthians 6:20
For God bought you with a high price. So you must honor God with your body.

GRAPPLE CHAT

Chat 1: Discover and explain how 1+1=1, according to 1 Corinthians.

Chat 2: Have you ever run a timed race? If so, what was that like?

Chat 3: Find in the Bible what sin you should "run away" from.

Chat 4: How many pairs of shoes do you have, and what are the different purposes of your pairs of shoes?

GRAPPLE CHALLENGE

Make a decision this week to run away from sexual sin—not to see how close to the line you can get without crossing over it.

NOTES:

_____

_____

_____

_____

_____

_____

_____

_____

THE "S" WORD

THEY REALLY THINK ABOUT *THAT*?

THE "S" WORD

They Really Think About *That*?
The Point: I Will Consider the Needs and Feelings of Others
The Passages: Romans 12:10, 16; 14:13; 15:7; Philippians 2:1-11

GET STARTED
Lesson 10. They Really Think About *That*?

GRAPPLE SCHEDULE

5 MINUTES	HANG TIME
10 MINUTES	GRAPPLE CHAT
10-15 MINUTES	GRAPPLE TIME
20-25 MINUTES	TEAM TIME
10 MINUTES	TEAM REPORTS
5 MINUTES	PRAYER & CHALLENGE

SUPPLIES
Bibles, Grapple DVD, DVD player, music CD, CD player, copy of the Grapple Team Guide for each person, paper, pens or pencils, bull's-eye

BIBLE BASIS FOR TEACHERS
The Passage: Philippians 2:1-11
This passage describes what having a Christ-like attitude looks like. These verses remind us not to selfishly look out only for our own interests, but to look out for the interests of others the way Jesus did. Even though Jesus is the Son of God, he gave up his divine privileges and came to earth to die a criminal's death on the cross for our sins. In the same way, when we consider the feelings of others, we may end up having to sacrifice some of our own needs.

How does this relate to the Grapple Question? Men and women are different. They think differently, react to things differently, and interact with each other differently. Guys and girls in junior high are just as different. Girls may dress a certain way because it's cool or everyone else seems to be doing it. Often girls are ignorant about how guys think when they look at girls dressed a certain way—it's helpful for girls to know. It's also helpful for guys to know what girls are thinking about when they act a certain way or say certain things. In this lesson, students will experience a safe environment where they can have an open dialogue about these issues. Teenagers will come to a better understanding of the opposite sex and will consider the feelings and needs of those they encounter every day.

How does this connect to Jesus? Paul encouraged Christians in Philippi to imitate Jesus. Jesus thought about others when he came to earth to accomplish his mission. Jesus didn't have to give up his rightful place as God, but he did: *"He gave up his divine privileges; he took the humble position of a slave and was born as a human being" (Philippians 2:7).* In the same manner, we must think of others—how they feel and what they think. When we consider the feelings of others, we'll be mindful about what we're wearing, how we're speaking, and what we're doing.

GRAPPLE HANG TIME: 5 MINUTES
Play music as kids enjoy snacks and friendship, and then play an opening countdown from the Grapple DVD to wrap up Grapple Hang Time.

GRAPPLE CHAT: 10 MINUTES
Have students form pairs; if you have an uneven number of kids, it's OK to have one trio in the mix. Ask each group to chat about two of the four topics below that relate to today's grapple topic. (Answers in parentheses are samples.)

IN PAIRS
Chat 1: Find out in the Bible whose attitude ours should resemble. (Jesus' attitude, Philippians 2:5)

Chat 2: Have you ever been hypnotized? If so, describe the experience. If not, what do you think the experience would be like?

Chat 3: Discover what one name someday will cause everyone to bow. (Jesus, Philippians 2:10)

Chat 4: What's your favorite flavor of ice cream? Do you meet many people who have the same favorite flavor as you?

GRAPPLE TIME: 10-15 MINUTES
Get Ready: Separate guys and girls into different groups, if you have a mixed-gender group of teenagers. Within groups, have students form pairs. Cue the Grapple DVD to the "What They're Thinking!" clip.

It's a question most guys ask: What do girls think about? Girls ask the same question about guys. And if we're really brave we ask: What does the opposite sex think about, well, sex?

Today let's be brave.

I have answers to that question. They're answers based on research, but that doesn't mean they're true for everyone. They're just mostly true, most of the time, for most people.

I'll announce a research finding and you, with your partner, will decide if you think it's true or false. The catch: You and your partner must agree on your answer—so talk it over for about 60 seconds before you vote. Ready?

Finding #1: All guys think about is sex. True or false? Talk it over. In 60 seconds I'll ask for a vote.

After 60 seconds repeat the finding and ask for a show of hands for "true" and then "false."

It's false. Guys do think about sex more often than girls—but it's not all they think about! One study found that 54 percent of men think about sex several times a day, and only 19 percent of women do.

Finding #2: Girls are more complicated when it comes to romantic attraction than guys. True or false? Talk with your partner. You'll vote in 60 seconds.

After 60 seconds take a vote.

It's true. It's much harder to figure out what girls find attractive. Some researchers aren't sure even the girls know!

Finding #3: Guys want sex. Girls want romance. True or false?

After 60 seconds take a vote.

False. One study found 80 percent of 16-year-old boys date girls primarily because they like the person. Guys want relationships, too!

TELL ALL
Share which finding you thought was the most surprising, and why.

We're not the only ones who are surprised by what the opposite sex is thinking. Check out this video clip.

Show the "What They're Thinking!" clip on the Grapple DVD.

IN PAIRS
What's something you'd like to know about how the opposite sex thinks?

Bad news: You can't read minds. Good news: You can build relationships, and people will tell you what they think. What's the opposite sex thinking? Let's grapple with that today.

GRAPPLE TEAM TIME: 20-25 MINUTES
Break into Grapple Teams. Encourage Grapple Team leaders to check in with kids about their week. Grapple Team leaders will facilitate discussion, using the Grapple Team Guide on pages 99-101. Afterward, students will report what they learned.

GRAPPLE TEAM REPORTS: 10 MINUTES

At the end of Grapple Team Time, match Grapple Teams that chose Option 1 with Grapple Teams that chose Option 2 from page 101. Have teams present their reports.

(If you have an uneven number of teams, simply form one group of three teams for the presentations. If you have only two Grapple Teams, simply do the presentations one team at a time.)

GRAPPLE PRAYER AND CHALLENGE: 5 MINUTES

Read the Grapple Prayer options. Have the class choose one prayer option that everyone will do. Allow students time to pray about what they discovered. Then close in prayer.

Get Ready: For Option 2, affix the bull's-eye to the far wall, and distribute paper to students.

Option 1: Little and Big

Think of "little" sins from this past week that you might have thought were too insignificant to confess. Confess these to God, and ask God to help you change your attitude about all sin—even the "little" sins.

Option 2: Marksman, Markswoman

Make paper airplanes, and take turns throwing the airplanes at the bull's-eye. Walk to wherever your airplane lands and pray to God about one way you miss the mark in your life. Relate what you say to what you learned today.

GRAPPLE CHALLENGE

I encourage and challenge you to see members of the opposite sex first and foremost as people God loves. Guys and girls may be different in many ways, but we're all alike in at least two ways: We want to be loved, and we are loved— by God. As you move deeper into relationships with the opposite sex, seek healthy friendships. Build friendships that keep sex in the proper perspective and friendships that encourage and uplift—not use—the other person. Ask God to give you a heart that seeks what's best for others, not just what's best for yourself.

WEEKLY GRAPPLE CONNECTION

Grapple Question: They Really Think About That?
Kids Learn: I Will Consider the Needs and Feelings of Others
Dig Into the Bible: Philippians 2:1-11

As teenagers grow, so does their curiosity about the opposite sex. And that's not surprising, because God created men and women to be very different from each other. You know that your child is in for a lifetime of discovering how the minds of the opposite sex work!

Tonight might be a good time to have a lighthearted dinner-table discussion about the differences between guys and girls. Ask your kids to share their experiences about how people of each gender think, react, attract, and express themselves. Make sure to share what you've learned in your own friendships and relationships.

End your discussion by reminding your family that guys and girls may be different in many ways, but we're all alike in at least two ways: We want to be loved, and we are loved—by God. Encourage your teenager to act, dress, and speak in a way that honors God. Pray together, asking God to give your family members a heart for others that seeks their best at all times—just as God desires the best for each of you.

- -

GRAPPLE TEAM GUIDE LESSON 10
In your Grapple Team, use this guide to grapple with today's question.

Whether you're a guy or a girl, you'll have far better relationships if you view the opposite sex as more than a collection of body parts or an unreal fantasy. Consider the needs and feelings of others and discover what they're thinking. List ways you might do that as you relate with the opposite sex.

_____

_____

_____

_____

_____

Share your answers. Together, rate each answer this way:
1. Winner—great way to find out what someone's thinking.
2. Maybe—it might be a good idea.
3. Nope—this idea is really about you, not others.

Read Philippians 2:1-4

List below any helpful insights you find for building a relationship with the opposite sex and discovering what they're thinking.

_____

_____

_____

_____

_____

Rate the answers above with the same scale you used earlier. How do the suggestions stack up?

Note: That may be great dating advice, but you just read a description of Jesus' attitude in reaching out to you. He considers your needs and feelings, respects your thoughts, and wants a friendship with you.

Read Philippians 2:5-11

IN PAIRS

How do you know, really, that Jesus values you? He humbled himself—set aside his status and power so he could connect with and serve you. Who wouldn't want to have a friend like that—and pour out his or her heart to such a friend? When you have this sort of attitude toward guys, girls, everyone, you'll find out what they're thinking. They'll tell you because they'll trust you. And you'll be worthy of the trust. When have you seen this work in your own relationships?

There's no mystery about what guys think—or what girls think. There's a mystery about what people think—and some great advice in the Bible about building relationships where it's safe to share.

Read Romans 12:10, 16; 14:13; 15:7

Jot the advice you find in these verses:

_____

_____

_____

_____

How could you use what you just discovered—today?

GRAPPLE TEAM REPORTS
With your team, choose one of the options below to report what you discovered.

Option 1: Knowit Poets!
Write a poem or a rap about what you learned today, making every sentence contain the word others.

Option 2: Dialogue
Create a scene from your everyday life that includes dialogue involving everyone on your team (or several sample conversations) to demonstrate what you've learned today.

THEY REALLY THINK ABOUT THAT?
(STUDENT)

1 Corinthians 6:20
For God bought you with a high price. So you must honor God with your body.

GRAPPLE CHAT

Chat 1: Find out in the Bible whose attitude ours should resemble.

Chat 2: Have you ever been hypnotized? If so, describe the experience. If not, what do you think the experience would be like?

Chat 3: Discover what one name someday will cause everyone to bow.

Chat 4: What's your favorite flavor of ice cream? Do you meet many people who have the same favorite flavor as you?

GRAPPLE CHALLENGE

As you encounter members of the opposite sex this week, think about them first as people who are loved by God.

NOTES:

_____

_____

_____

_____

_____

_____

_____

_____

_____

THE "S" WORD

WHY IS IT SO WRONG?

THE "S" WORD

Why Is It So Wrong?
The Point: God Created Me to Enjoy Sex
The Passages: Genesis 2:18-25; Deuteronomy 5:18; Proverbs 5:18-19; Song of Songs 8:6-7; Matthew 15:19-20; 1 Corinthians 6:15-16; 7:2-4; 10:13

GET STARTED
Lesson 11. Why Is It So Wrong?

GRAPPLE SCHEDULE

5 MINUTES	HANG TIME
10 MINUTES	GRAPPLE CHAT
10-15 MINUTES	GRAPPLE TIME
20-25 MINUTES	TEAM TIME
10 MINUTES	TEAM REPORTS
5 MINUTES	PRAYER & CHALLENGE

SUPPLIES
Bibles, Grapple DVD, DVD player, music CD, CD player, copy of the Grapple Team Guide for each person, paper, pens or pencils, colored markers

BIBLE BASIS FOR TEACHERS
The Passage: Genesis 2:18-25
Adam's need for a mate—someone to stand alongside him—didn't come as a surprise to God. The parade of animals for Adam to name had a purpose beyond the naming: It pointed out to Adam that he was alone and that he didn't have a mate like him, someone with whom he could share his life. Adam needed someone to commence the procreation of humanity with him. After helping Adam come to this realization, God created woman.

Many appropriate conclusions have been drawn from Eve's being created from Adam's rib (from his side), such as the intent that they work side by side, that they be equal to each other in standing before God, and that they be "united into one" in the bond of marriage. Without Eve, Adam was incomplete. And without Adam, Eve wouldn't have existed. Both had strengths and weaknesses. But together, man and woman became a whole being, able to stand together and support each other, just as God had planned from the start.

How does this relate to the Grapple Question? After being told over and over again about the "evils" of sex, teenagers can either become jaded about the whole issue, or they can conclude that sex is bad and should be avoided at all costs. For this lesson, students will grapple with whether sex is a good thing or a bad thing. From the very beginning, man and woman were created to enjoy each other. What's the difference between sexual immorality and sex the way God intended it to be?

How does this connect to Jesus? Jesus came to give us all *"a rich and satisfying life" (John 10:10)*. Part of a satisfying life is enjoying God's gift of sex. But we are to enjoy it when and how God intended. In the right context—namely marriage—sex is a gift and blessing. Pursued outside of that context, sex can be destructive. When we have sex outside of marriage, we become emotionally and spiritually connected to the wrong people, for the wrong reasons, at the wrong time.

GRAPPLE HANG TIME: 5 MINUTES
Play music as kids enjoy snacks and friendship, and then play an opening countdown from the Grapple DVD to wrap up Grapple Hang Time.

GRAPPLE CHAT: 10 MINUTES
Have students form pairs; if you have an uneven number of kids, it's OK to have one trio in the mix. Ask each group to chat about two of the four topics below that relate to today's grapple topic. (Answers in parentheses are samples.)

IN PAIRS
Chat 1: Find out in the Bible what was worn on the first date. (Nothing! Genesis 2:25)

Chat 2: What are the names of every pet you currently own or have ever owned?

Chat 3: Discover who the first Assistant Gardener was. (Eve, Genesis 2:18)

Chat 4: Who are you named after? Do you know of anyone who is named after you?

GRAPPLE TIME: 10-15 MINUTES
Get Ready: Cue the Grapple DVD to the "Keeping Up With the Joneses" clip. For this activity you'll need sheets of paper and colored markers. Give a fistful of markers and a couple of sheets of paper to each Grapple Team.

Congratulations! You've just been hired by the Focal Point Advertising Agency. You've been assigned the task of creating an ad for the Sexual Self-Control Council.

The Council encourages unmarried teenagers not to have sex. But teenagers and adults are both asking: Why is sex before marriage so wrong?

Your ad should give reasons not to have sex before marriage. Take a few minutes to talk about what your ad might say. Jot some notes. If you want to sketch out your ad, feel free.

Did I mention the client will come back in five minutes to see your ideas? Get started!

Play music while Grapple Teams work. Circulate and offer encouragement. Be sure everyone is participating. When there's one minute left, announce that the client is due back in 60 seconds. When time is up, turn off the music and ask each Grapple Team to present its ad.

IN PAIRS
Of the reasons mentioned not to have sex as a teenager, which one seemed most convincing to you? Why? And why is sex wrong for unmarried people?

TELL ALL
Share your conclusions with the larger group.

Here's a video that digs a bit deeper into the "S" word.

Show the "Keeping Up With the Joneses" clip on the Grapple DVD.

It sometimes seems like a cruel joke: God creates you to enjoy sex but then tells you that you can't do it yet. What's up with that? Why is sex before marriage so wrong? Let's grapple with that.

Collect ads and display them in your meeting area.

GRAPPLE TEAM TIME: 20-25 MINUTES
Break into Grapple Teams. Encourage Grapple Team leaders to check in with kids about their week. Grapple Team leaders will facilitate discussion, using the Grapple Team Guide on pages 111-112. Afterward, students will report what they learned.

GRAPPLE TEAM REPORTS: 10 MINUTES
At the end of Grapple Team Time, match Grapple Teams that chose Option 1 with Grapple Teams that chose Option 2 from page 112. Have teams present their reports.

(If you have an uneven number of teams, simply form one group of three teams for the presentations. If you have only two Grapple Teams, simply do the presentations one team at a time.)

GRAPPLE PRAYER AND CHALLENGE: 5 MINUTES
Read the Grapple Prayer options. Have the class choose one prayer option that everyone will do. Allow students time to pray about what they discovered. Then close in prayer.

Get Ready: For Option 1, make sure students have paper and pens or pencils.

Option 1: Prayer Pile

Get in a circle with the rest of your group. Write a prayer to God. Then crumple up the paper with the prayer on it and make a pile of crumpled papers in the middle of the circle. Choose one crumpled prayer from the pile. Silently pray the words written on the paper, and then ask God to answer the prayer for the person who wrote it.

Option 2: Lectio Divina

Get comfortable, preferably sitting apart from each other. Read a Bible passage aloud, and then remain in silence for a few minutes and think about the verses. Close your eyes and breathe deeply. Then read aloud Romans 8:35-39, slowly and with feeling. Then read it two more times the same way. Finally, allow a few minutes to silently bask in God's love.

GRAPPLE CHALLENGE

I encourage and challenge you to stay faithful to God's plan for sex. God designed us to enjoy sex. If we enjoy it when and how God intended, sex is a gift and a blessing. But if we pursue it anywhere else, it can be destructive. We become emotionally and spiritually connected to the wrong people for the wrong reasons at the wrong time. And any—or all—of the things you captured on your ads can happen. God designed you to enjoy sex. God also designed you to wait for the right time. I want you to find encouragement in these words from 1 Corinthians 10:13. "The temptations in your life are no different from what others experience. And God is faithful. He will not allow the temptation to be more than you can stand. When you are tempted, he will show you a way out so that you can endure."

WEEKLY GRAPPLE CONNECTION

Grapple Question: Why Is It So Wrong?
Kids Learn: God Created Me to Enjoy Sex
Dig Into the Bible: Genesis 2:18-25

It sometimes seems like a cruel joke: God creates us to enjoy sex but then tells us not to do it before marriage. In a culture where the media and your child's peers say it's OK to have sex whenever it feels right, how do you instill God's sexual values in your teenager?

Pick up a teen magazine on your way home tonight. Then spend a few minutes flipping through it with your teenager. Rip out pages that send any kind of sexual message, and lay them around you in a circle on the floor. Then talk about what it feels like to be surrounded by those messages. What effect does it have on your thoughts when you see those advertisements all around? What are some ways to stay pure in the midst of all of those sexual messages?

The problem isn't with sex—it's with timing. Outside marriage, sex is self-destructive and hurts others. God created us to enjoy sex in a marriage relationship. Encourage your teenager to stay faithful to God's plan for sex.

Every morning this week, pray for your teenager's ability to abstain from sex until marriage.

- -

GRAPPLE TEAM GUIDE LESSON 11

In your Grapple Team, use this guide to grapple with today's question.

No question about it: Sex is great stuff. It should be: God created it! Still have doubts? Read for yourself.

Read Genesis 2:18-25

IN PAIRS

What does it mean to be united into one? Why was the woman the final necessary component for God's creation to be good?

Look up and paraphrase the following passages:

Read Proverbs 5:18-19

_____

Read Song of Songs 8:6-7

_____

Read 1 Corinthians 7:2-4

_____

God paints a beautiful picture of sex. Warm. Intimate. Passionate. Bonding. But a different picture comes into focus when the Bible describes sex outside of marriage.

Look up these passages. In your Grapple Team, discuss the impact of sex in these situations:

Read Deuteronomy 5:18; Matthew 15:19-20; and 1 Corinthians 6:15-16

IN PAIRS

When experienced outside marriage, sex is far darker than when enjoyed inside marriage. The problem isn't with sex—it's with timing. What are other things you can think of that are good when done at one time but bad when done at another?

Share your ideas with your Grapple Team.

Why do you think God wired us to enjoy something we have to wait to enjoy? Think about your ads—what would you suggest an unmarried teenager do to avoid having sex before it's the right time?

_____

_____

_____

GRAPPLE TEAM REPORTS

With your team, choose one of the options below to report what you discovered.

Option 1: Top 5

Create a Top 5 list of the most important, challenging, or meaningful things you learned today. Be prepared to explain why each item on the list is so important, challenging, or meaningful.

Option 2: Text It

Write a 140-character text message that you could send to a friend or family member explaining what you learned today.

WHY IS IT SO WRONG?
(STUDENT)

1 Corinthians 6:20
For God bought you with a high price. So you must honor God with your body.

GRAPPLE CHAT
Chat 1: Find out in the Bible what was worn on the first date.

Chat 2: What are the names of every pet you currently own or have ever owned?

Chat 3: Discover who the first Assistant Gardener was.

Chat 4: Who are you named after? Do you know of anyone who is named after you?

GRAPPLE CHALLENGE
Remind yourself this week that God gave sex to you as a gift, and God wants you to enjoy it. God just wants you to wait for the right time and place: marriage.

NOTES:

_____

_____

_____

_____

_____

_____

_____

_____

_____

THE "S" WORD

IS DIVORCE OK?

THE "S" WORD

Is Divorce OK?
The Point: Marriage Consists of Love, Commitment, and Mutual Submission
The Passages: Malachi 2:16; Matthew 19:3-9; Luke 11:4; Ephesians 4:32; 5:21-33; 1 John 1:8-9

GET STARTED
Lesson 12. Is Divorce OK?

GRAPPLE SCHEDULE

5 MINUTES	HANG TIME
10 MINUTES	GRAPPLE CHAT
10-15 MINUTES	GRAPPLE TIME
20-25 MINUTES	TEAM TIME
10 MINUTES	TEAM REPORTS
5 MINUTES	PRAYER & CHALLENGE

SUPPLIES
Bibles, Grapple DVD, DVD player, music CD, CD player, copy of the Grapple Team Guide for each person, paper, pens or pencils, a bath towel, a carpeted surface or a throw rug, 20 playing cards for each Grapple Team

BIBLE BASIS FOR TEACHERS
The Passage: Ephesians 5:21-33
These verses tell wives to submit to their husbands and husbands to love their wives. This passage often offends people who feel that the word *submit* is effectively making women seem weak or powerless in comparison with men. However, when looking at this passage in light of Christ and his love for the church, we see that God values men and women equally. God's intent in this comparison is for women to love and serve their husbands and for men to love and serve their wives, just as Christ loved and served his bride, the church. Paul encouraged husbands and wives to respect each other and be submissive to each other mutually. When respect and love break down, relationships and marriages suffer.

How does this relate to the Grapple Question? Many junior highers today have parents who are divorced, who are going through divorce, or who will go through a divorce at some time in the future. Sometimes churches inform these kids that their parents are disobeying God. Other times, churches avoid the topic altogether. The truth, however, is that dealing with divorce is difficult for everyone involved. For this lesson, students will grapple with what mutual respect and mutual submission look like. Is divorce OK in cases where mutual respect breaks down or is destroyed? What about marital unfaithfulness? What constitutes marital unfaithfulness? Divorce is a tough topic, and this lesson will help teenagers sort out some of the issues that surround this tragedy.

How does this connect to Jesus? Jesus taught about divorce and condemned it except for cases of adultery. Jesus understood that divorce causes extreme rifts in relationships and families and is very painful. Paul affirmed that marriage is to be set upon a foundation of love, commitment, and mutual submission— principles that Christ himself taught. Divorce is often a direct result of the couple violating those principles. The Bible teaches Christians to embrace the principles of love and be encouraged to avoid divorce, which causes so much pain and suffering.

GRAPPLE HANG TIME: 5 MINUTES

Play music as kids enjoy snacks and friendship, and then play an opening countdown from the Grapple DVD to wrap up Grapple Hang Time.

GRAPPLE CHAT: 10 MINUTES

Have students form pairs; if you have an uneven number of kids, it's OK to have one trio in the mix. Ask each group to chat about two of the four topics below that relate to today's grapple topic. (Answers in parentheses are samples.)

IN PAIRS

Chat 1: Discover who Jesus has in mind when he hums "Here Comes the Bride." (Us—the church, Ephesians 5:23)

Chat 2: Have you ever broken a bone? Which bone(s) did you break? How did it happen?

Chat 3: Find this comparison in the Bible: <u>Husbands</u> love and serve their <u>wives</u>, just as <u>Jesus</u> loves and serves _____. (The church, Ephesians 5:25)

Chat 4: Why is divorce such a messy, painful experience?

GRAPPLE TIME: 10-15 MINUTES

Get Ready: Cue the Grapple DVD to the "Divorce?" clip. Give each Grapple team up to 20 playing cards. Assign each team a different surface on which to work: a carpeted surface (or a throw rug on the floor); a smooth surface (tile or slick table top); or a bath towel held in place off the ground, stretched tight and steady.

Just one Grapple Team? Use the bath towel as a foundation.

Here's your assignment: Build a card tower as tall as possible in four minutes. The rules:
- *No gluing, licking, taping, or otherwise sticking cards together.*
- *Your tower must be freestanding.*
- *You must all participate in building the tower.*
- *You must build on the surface you were assigned.*

Ready? Go!

Give a 30-second warning when time is running out.

Invite teams to compare towers.

IN TEAMS
Talk about what worked for or against you in building your tower. What gave some teams an advantage or a disadvantage?

Ask teams to share their observations.

Clearly, having the right foundation matters. If your foundation was shaky, you had no chance. That's true for towers. It's true for marriages, too.

IN PAIRS
What are some things that help a marriage have a solid foundation? Explain. What keeps marriages from having a solid foundation?

TELL ALL
Share your observations.

Let's watch a video clip that dives deeper into this subject.

Show the "Divorce?" clip on the Grapple DVD.

Not every marriage survives. Some experts say nearly half of all marriages end in divorce. Is divorce OK? Let's grapple with that.

GRAPPLE TEAM TIME: 20-25 MINUTES
Break into Grapple Teams. Encourage Grapple Team leaders to check in with kids about their week. Grapple Team leaders will facilitate discussion, using the Grapple Team Guide on pages 121-122. Afterward, students will report what they learned.

GRAPPLE TEAM REPORTS: 10 MINUTES
At the end of Grapple Team Time, match Grapple Teams that chose Option 1 with Grapple Teams that chose Option 2 from page 122. Have teams present their reports.

(If you have an uneven number of teams, simply form one group of three teams for the presentations. If you have only two Grapple Teams, simply do the presentations one team at a time.)

GRAPPLE PRAYER AND CHALLENGE: 5 MINUTES

Read the Grapple Prayer options. Have the class choose one prayer option that everyone will do. Allow students time to pray about what they discovered. Then close in prayer.

Option 1: Quiet Prayers

Spread out around the room, and get comfortable so you won't be distracted by others. Psalm 143:10 begins with, "Teach me to do your will." Pray that simple phrase over and over, slowly and quietly, and listen for what the Holy Spirit wants to teach you today. Write down any thoughts or ideas that come to mind as you listen.

Option 2: Letter Prayers

Write a letter to Jesus. Tell him what you know is true about him and what you're unsure about; ask for his strength and help in developing a deeper trust in him.

GRAPPLE CHALLENGE

I challenge you to do the things you can do now to develop into someone who can make and keep marriage vows—someone who knows, loves, and follows Jesus—and who's ready to build a marriage on a firm foundation.

You're building that foundation right now. How you handle relationships now sets the stage for how you'll handle them later. Be a person of your word now so you can be a person of your word later. Let God direct you in your friendships now so you'll know how to let God direct you in marriage later.

WEEKLY GRAPPLE CONNECTION

Grapple Question: Is Divorce OK?
Kids Learn: Marriage Consists of Love, Commitment, and Mutual Submission
Dig Into the Bible: Ephesians 5:21-33

Teenagers often worry about divorce—either that their parents will separate, or that they won't have what it takes to maintain their own future marriages. Make a list with your child of the top five things that a marriage needs to survive (such as commitment, trust, and love). Talk about the challenges of marriage, and encourage your teenager to practice those skills in his or her friendships and dating relationships now.

If your family has been through a divorce, it might be reassuring to your teenager to talk about what went wrong and what you learned from the experience. Romans 8:28 says, "And we know that God causes everything to work together for the good of those who love God and are called according to his purpose for them." God loves you and your teenager, and God can heal the pain and grief caused by divorce.

GRAPPLE TEAM GUIDE LESSON 12

In your Grapple Team, use this guide to grapple with today's question.

Our Grapple Question is this: Is divorce ever OK? Good question, but a better one might be: Does God say divorce is ever OK? After all, God's opinion matters—a lot!

Look up the following verses as a Grapple Team and answer this question: How does God feel about divorce?

Read Malachi 2:16 and Matthew 19:3-8

_____

_____

_____

_____

_____

_____

IN PAIRS

Share your answers. Then discuss the following list of reasons a couple might divorce. Do you know couples that have divorced because of one or more of these reasons? Would you get a divorce because of any of them? If so, which ones, and why? If not, why not?

___ The couple can't have children.
___ Someone is abusive.
___ Someone is an addict.
___ Someone is unfaithful.
___ Someone falls out of love with the other person.
___ One person wants to move; the other person doesn't.
___ Someone gets fat.

Read Matthew 19:9; Luke 11:4; and Ephesians 4:32

God isn't a fan of divorce, but Jesus mentioned a situation where divorce might be OK. Note: Couples aren't required to divorce if a husband or wife is unfaithful.

They could choose to do the hard, difficult work of forgiveness—and restore their marriage.

IN PAIRS
Many dating couples break up if either person even looks at someone else. Imagine the pain of your spouse looking—and then acting. No wonder it's hard to forgive. Could you forgive someone who cheated on you? Why or why not?

Read Matthew 19:9 and Ephesians 5:21-33

IN PAIRS
What exactly is cheating for a married couple? Having sex outside of marriage? Thinking about it? Not caring for each other thoughtfully? What does it mean to "submit to one another"?

Many people get divorced—with or without an OK reason. What do you think are the reasonable and appropriate consequences for couples that divorce?

Read 1 John 1:8-9

Divorce may be a sin, but it's a sin that God can forgive. And if God can forgive it, can't we?

GRAPPLE TEAM REPORTS
With your team, choose one of the options below to report what you discovered.

Option 1: ABCs
Write the ABCs of what you learned today: a statement that starts with an A, a statement that starts with a B, and so on. Try to go as far into the alphabet as you can—even all the way to Z.

Option 2: Relay Report
Discuss some of the big ideas you've learned today. Once you're ready to make your presentation to the other team, line up on one side of the room. Run down to the other end of the room and back. When you return, tell about something you learned today. Then the next person in line runs to the end of the room and back, and reports something else. Continue until everyone has participated.

IS DIVORCE OK?

(STUDENT)

1 Corinthians 6:20
For God bought you with a high price. So you must honor God with your body.

GRAPPLE CHAT

Chat 1: Discover who Jesus has in mind when he hums "Here Comes the Bride."

Chat 2: Have you ever broken a bone? Which bone(s) did you break? How did it happen?

Chat 3: Find this comparison in the Bible: <u>Husbands</u> love and serve their <u>wives</u>, just as <u>Jesus</u> loves and serves _____.

Chat 4: Why is divorce such a messy, painful experience?

GRAPPLE CHALLENGE

Give God control over your relationships this week, so God can be in control of your marriage in the future.

NOTES:

_____

_____

_____

_____

_____

_____

_____

_____

_____